ANCIENT
EGYPTIAN
MYSTICISM

ANCIENT EGYPTIAN MYSTICISM

AND ITS RELEVANCE TODAY

BY
JOHN VAN AUKEN

ARE
PRESS

ASSOCIATION FOR
RESEARCH AND
ENLIGHTENMENT

A.R.E. Press • Virginia Beach • Virginia

A.R.E. Press
215 67th Street
Virginia Beach, VA 23451-2061

Library of Congress Cataloging-in-Publication Data
Van Auken, John.
    Ancient Egyptian mysticism : and its relevance today / by John Van Auken.
        p.   cm.
    ISBN 0-87604-422-4 (pbk.)
    1. Egypt—Religion—Miscellanea.   2. Cayce, Edgar, 1877-1945.
I. Title.
BF1999.V296   1999
135'.45—dc21   99-11341

Cover design by Lightbourne Images

Contents

Introduction .... *vii*

1 God and the Godlings 1

2 Gods and Metaphor 13

3 Ra Ta: The Story of a High Priest 21

4 Images and Meanings 39

5 Temples and Bodies 45

6 Initiation 51

7 Mystical Anatomy: The Secret Parts of Our Being 57

8 The Great Pyramid: A Masterpiece of Mathematics and Mysticism 63

9 The Great Hall of Records 73

INTRODUCTION

My interest in Egypt was born of a mystical experience. I had been in a deep meditative state when a
part of my mind opened to a scene so real it felt as if
it were happening *live*. It was an ancient Egyptian altar ceremony, and somehow I was a part of it, a living part of it. You
may remember a long-running television show called *Quantum
Leap*, in which a time traveler, Dr. Samuel Beckett, "leaps" from
one lifetime to another. I felt I had leapt into an actual ancient
Egyptian life, not a memory, but an ancient life that somehow
still existed, though in a different time period than my current
one.

This experience so pressed against my conscious mind that I
had to learn more about Egypt. I went to the library, found a
private corner of my own, and thumbed through a dozen beautiful, fascinating books on Egypt. I was moved deeply. Latent
within me was a love and appreciation for ancient Egypt. As I

continued my studying, I developed a particular interest in Egyptian mythology and mysticism.

A short time after this initial experience, I had another one and then another. Some were during meditation, others were dreams, and a few were flashes before my mind's eye. The experiences were too real to ignore or dismiss. I was learning more from them than the many books I read.

Eventually, I was on an airplane to Egypt. I traveled throughout Egypt, visiting all the pyramids, temples, and tombs with the well-known guide, Ahmed Fayed, who handled all of the Egypt tours for Edgar Cayce's organization, the Association for Research and Enlightenment, Inc. (A.R.E.). Ahmed knew exactly what I was interested in—not the art, architecture, politics, dynasties, or history, but the mystical, mythological stories and, wherever possible, the records of actual mystical ceremonies.

In the sacred temple at Abydos, the Jerusalem or Mecca of ancient Egypt, I asked Ahmed if my group could sit in the chamber dedicated to Osiris and meditate for a while. He was accommodating. We sat on the hard, cold, stone floor in this very special chamber and began to still our minds and bodies. The guards at the temple were laughing and talking, the echo of their voices was so great inside the temple that it was very difficult to meditate. However, rather than give up or get angry I asked myself, "When was I ever going to get back to this temple?" I had to succeed then. I tried with all my might to filter out their voices and get into deep meditation. It worked. It worked so well that I not only lost consciousness of them, I completely lost consciousness of the temple and my group, entering again into a vivid ancient Egyptian ceremony. This time, it was an initiation ceremony involving water and fire.

I found myself standing shoulder-deep in a pool of holy water, naked. I knew it was a purification ritual. As I walked up the stone steps out of this sacred pool, attending priests wrapped a floor-length cape around me. Then, they anointed my head with oil and combed my hair back. My hair was black and thick with oil. Two of them approached and handed me the two scepters of Egypt, the crook and the flail. Somehow, I intuitively knew that if I wanted to move, I held them out in front of me; to stop, I crossed them close to my chest. I looked up and held them out in front of me, causing me to glide across the floor, not walk, glide just an inch above the floor. In front of me were two long rows of priests and gods. One row on my left and the other on my right. I glided between them. They nodded their heads in approval. At least at first I thought this was in approval; as I nodded back I realized that it was also a nod of encouragement to continue through the next initiation. I looked up ahead of them to see what it was. To my amazement and concern, it was the sun, the real sun. At the end of this gantlet of priests and gods, I was to willingly enter Ra. But Ra was the real sun. I became very concerned that I would be burned if I entered the solar disk. I looked hard into the eyes of the priests and gods, expressing to them with my eyes my deep concern about this part of the initiation. They smiled and nodded with more enthusiasm than before. I knew that all I had to do was cross the scepters and I would stop. But, some knowing within me kept the scepters pointed straight for the fiery sun. As I entered it, I felt the searing heat, but instead of burning me, it cleansed me! The solar heat was burning away all my sins and weaknesses but not harming the rest of me. I began to draw its warmth into me, inhaling it, wanting more of it. It felt wonderful. I wanted it to burn me completely, thoroughly, until I was fully cleansed.

Suddenly, someone grabbed my arm and began shaking me saying, "John, wake up, we're going to miss our boat. We have to go. Wake up." I struggled to see through the sun's light. Two faces were staring at me, Ahmed and my colleague Kevin. I asked, "Who are you?" They both looked at each other and then turned to me and ordered me to get up and follow them closely without alarming the guards and others in our group. I obeyed, gradually realizing that I was supposed to be a part of this tour group, yet half of me was still in the initiation ceremony. Once on the bus, I fell back into the solar cleansing. It felt so good.

For most of my life I have budgeted time each day for meditation. I have studied and practiced several different techniques, becoming quite adept. The technique I used in the Abydos temple was developed by the famous Bible-reading seer Edgar Cayce. It was designed to help a three-dimensional mind open to the other dimensions and to move through them to a state of oneness which encompassed all the dimensions. Somehow, I was able to "leap" into living experiences that seemed to be occurring in another dimension of time and space. Unlike the fictional Dr. Samuel Beckett, I was always able to return to this time and space and to remain relatively normal, though strongly influenced by the experiences.

After the Abydos experience, I could look at a papyrus or temple wall and understand what I was seeing. I did not know the dynasty or the political characters, but I understood the mystical significance of the scene and its meaning to a priest or initiate. Fortunately, Ahmed was tolerant of my interpretations, at times even appreciative. He had been trained to read hieroglyphs and knew all the dynasties and characters, but he liked my strange mystical spin on the scenes carved or painted on the walls and papyri. We became good friends and teamed up to do more than a dozen A.R.E. tours of Egypt.

Eventually, I met some of the key archaeologists/ Egyptologists and learned about their discoveries and excavations. Each of them was as taken with Egypt as I was.

I actually began writing this book before my first trip to Egypt, but it really came together after touring Egypt and meeting so many others who love ancient Egypt. I hope this book conveys some of the wonder and wisdom of that great period in humanity's journey.

I could not have completed this book without the work of many others. I want to thank Ahmed Fayed, Dr. Zahi Hawass, Dr. Mark Lehner, Hugh Lynn Cayce, Rufus Mosely, Rebecca Ghittino, Ann Clapp, Mae Gimbert St. Clair, Ellen Cayce, Riley Simmons, William "Bill" Fix, Adrian Gilbert, Robert Bauval, John Anthony West, Graham Hancock, David Davidson, H. Aldersmith, and of course, Sir Wallis Budge, who translated *The Egyptian Book of the Dead*, and Marsham Adams, who retranslated it, giving it the wonderfully mystical title, *The Book of the Master of the Hidden Places*. I also thank my patient wife, Doris, and supportive children, James, Jacqueline, and Evan, for enduring so many of my long trips away from home.

1

GOD AND THE GODLINGS

I f evolution is the only view of life, then there is little reason
to look back to an ancient culture for wisdom and insight.
According to evolutionary theory, everything old is primitive. If, on the other hand, we come to know that before this
great evolution of ours, there was a great involution into matter,
then there is much to be learned from looking back. This is why
ancient Egypt is worth studying. Its picture stories contain remnants from an important time in the lives of our souls.

As *souls*, not physical humans, we descended from higher
realms and higher states of consciousness during an involution
into matter. As we separated from the higher realms, we gradually lost consciousness of them, focusing increasingly on this
physical dimension. Some among the soul group realized that
we were heading into a more limiting condition, so they recorded important stories and information that would help us
rise again to the glory that was ours before the physical world

was. A plan was developed. The way in and out of this realm was recorded, but cryptically, so that only those who sought it for the right reasons could find it. The manuscript that we now call *The Egyptian Book of the Dead* actually carries the hieroglyphic title, *The Book of the Master of the Hidden Places*. It is not a death-ritual book as so many today believe but an inner map used to guide the soul back through the inner darkness to the light of the higher dimensions, which few seek to find. It was written because our descent was progressing rapidly; soon we'd have no memory of the former places from whence we came.

The story of our creation, fall, banishment, and long, slow journey home is recorded in many sacred books in many cultures. There's a pattern to all souls' journeys. For example, the pattern in the Jewish, Christian, and Islamic theology, as described in our Scriptures, goes like this:

> Creation of God's children in God's image.
> Creation of humans in flesh.
> Fall of humankind (through disobedience).
> Loss of the Garden (contact with God).
> Suffering and seeking.
> Inspiration.
> Promise from God.
> Victory over the oppressor (physical focus).
> Freedom from bondage (physical desire).
> Covenant with God.
> Rejuvenation and reconnection in the mount.
> Building the new temple.
> Reconnect with God.

In most of the legends, as in this Jewish-Christian-Islamic one, this initial pattern was followed by a falling away again, which required a second or new pattern but with much of the key elements of the first.

> Falling away again.
> Loss of the Temple.
> Into bondage again.
> Suffering and seeking again.

Reinspiration.
A promise from God.
Victory over the oppressor.
Freedom from bondage again.
A new covenant with God.
Rejuvenation and reconnection in the mount.
Rebuilding of the temple.
Reconnect with God.

Again and again this pattern repeats itself. We see it in the early stories in Genesis about the Garden, Cain and Abel, and the journey from Seth to Enoch. We see it in the journey from Noah to Joseph. Again we see it in greater detail in the story of Moses and Joshua coming out of Egypt (bondage), crossing the desert (suffering and seeking), living at the foot of Mt. Sinai (rejuvenation and reconnection with things spiritual), and finally entering into the Promised Land. Then again in Saul, David, and Solomon. Again in the journey from Daniel to Jeshua, and the rebuilding of the Temple. The pattern repeats and repeats and repeats until a major change occurs: the coming of the Messiah.

Then, as seen in the Christian story, the Temple moves from its external place to an internal place within each of us. It moves from the outer physical world to the inner mental-spiritual world. After much testing and suffering, victory is fully realized and the temple is resurrected to life eternal. It is also seen in The Revelation where, after much struggle and rebirthing, Satan is bound, the Garden is regained, a new heaven and a new earth come, the Holy City and Temple are come like a new bride, and the Tree of Life is once again ours, forever—coming full circle from the loss of these things in the Garden of Genesis.

This same pattern is found in ancient Egyptian teachings, thousands of years before the tribes of Israel. In *The Egyptian Book of the Dead*, we find references to the creation of gods and humans: "One is the maker of the substance of the gods and of mankind." There are references to the "sound of those that rejoice in the mighty temple." There are references to a rebellion which will never be tolerated again: "the sons of the impotent revolt, never again shall they rise up!" Just as our theology uses the serpent as a symbol of the evil one, so are there ancient

Egyptian references to a struggle with the evil enemy in the form of a serpent: "May I crush the evil one, may I destroy the great serpent at his moment." There are shouts of victory over the evil one, even using the imagery of binding him, as The Revelation does, "Thine great enemy is given to the fire, the evil one hath fallen, he is bound." Even references to the coming of the Messiah, using the Christian symbolism of the fish, can be found: "May I see the abtu fish at his season of coming into existence." And these amazing descriptions of this great one: "the boy mighty, the heir of eternity, he begot and he gave birth to himself, the king of earth, this prince of the netherland, president of the mountains, coming forth from the water, drawing himself from the primal mother, nursing himself, increasing his limbs. O god of life, lord of love, all the peoples live when thou shinest, O crowned as king of the gods." There are also many references to one's own resurrection, such as, "May I see the coming forth of my soul." This clearly indicates a belief that the physical self has within it the soul-self.

When we realize where we, as souls, have been and what we, as souls, have done, we'll know better where we are headed and what we are in need of doing. We will also get a view into the truer nature of our being. "Know thyself," the old adage goes. Well, we are, were, and will be again, much more than physical Earthlings.

Our souls have traveled throughout the cosmos from the beginning of creation. Many of us, our souls, went through the initiations of these ancient mystery schools and temples during the thousands of years of descent into matter. Our souls have been impregnated with the messages and meanings of the strange images on the walls of these temples and tombs. As we reawaken the soul-self within us, we will remember and understand. It is hoped that, as we look at the images and ideas in this book, we will awaken memories that have been locked in our hearts for a very long time. This is one of the great aspects of this new era which we are entering, *an awakening*—an awakening like none other, where whole groups of souls rise to a more universal, eternal view of life, past and future.

Before we proceed, it's important to realize that ancient Egypt lasted an incredibly long time, much longer than we are accustomed to hearing about. If we use the datings that have recently been indicated by star alignments and metaphysical sources, it lasted somewhere between ten and eleven thousand years. Portions of *The Egyptian Book of the Dead* date from as early as the very first dynasty to as late as A.D. 200. However, the purer, truer teachings were more clearly held in the earliest times. As the involution went on, many of the godly, deeper truths were contaminated with ideas of the evolving human who, because of limited awareness or self-interest, distorted them or simply was not aware of the real teachings. Therefore, in the lore of ancient Egypt we will often find the same teaching or story told in different ways with different implications. It is best to consider the older one as the truer one. That is the way I have approached all of this material.

One God, Many Godlings

In these earliest times, the many gods of the Egyptians were unique children of One Great God, the Source of All Life. Among the many gods, none of them was considered to be the ultimate god. Each was a free-willed portion of the Great Oneness which composed the Most High God. Even in Genesis the plural form is used as the name of God, indicating that the One was composed of the many, and the many contained the Universal, Omnipresent One.

Ra, as great a god as he was to the ancient Egyptians, was not the ultimate deity, but a projection from out of the Ultimate Unseen One. The unindividuated Most High God would be considered the pure disk, symbolizing God's *unindividualized* nature. God was seen through Its creation—not directly, for It was not seeable as an individual[1]—but very similar to St. John's concept expressed in his epistle, "No man has at any time seen God . . . but the Begotten of God has revealed Him."[2]

Before the creation, the ancient Egyptian god *Nun* (or Nu)

---

[1] I am using the neutral pronoun *It* to avoid a male or female connotation of God. This God is whole, containing both sexual aspects within Itself. Furthermore, It is not personified, as "Him" or "Her" would imply.

[2] 1 John 4:12, 9.

was all there was. Nun is Infinity, Nothing, Nowhere, and Darkness. In Genesis, Nun would correspond to the verse, "darkness was upon the deep," which is followed by "let there be light." Within the Darkness, the god *Atum* (or Tem, or Tum) was self-created and began the creation from within itself. Atum literally means *not to be,* meaning unmanifested, not personified, not born. As written in the papyrus *Pepi I,* this was "spirit, still and formless, who bore within itself the sum of all existence."

This is similar to the Hindu descriptions of *Brahman* and *Atman.* According to the Hindus, God has two aspects: one is the unmanifested, unmoved, unchanged, the same yesterday, today, and tomorrow *(Brahman);* the other is present, active, and with us *(Atman).*[3] Atman is similar to the concept of the Logos, or "The Word," or "First Begotten of God," which begins St. John's Gospel and by which "all things were made."

Nun and Atum could be considered the feminine and masculine aspects of God. Nun is the womb of Mother God, dark, silent, yet latent with the potential for creation. Atum is the projected aspect of Father God, actively involved in and with the creation.

There are several texts in which the ancient Egyptian writers are clearly speaking of a singular God. Their apparent polytheism is due to their proximity to the original creation in which the created and the Creator were still one. The God had given birth to many godlings. The original, wiser, ancient Egyptians were not polytheistic, as the following examples indicate. But later, as the enlightenment was lost, there are indications that this changed. Here are examples of the One God concepts. This first example recalls Genesis's teaching that we were created in the image of God and Jesus' teaching[4] that we are gods.

> *Thou hast received the form of God, because of this Thou hast become great before the gods. This Pepi is, therefore, a god, the son of the God.*[5]

---

[3] Interesting how similar *Atum* is to *Atman,* and to the Hebrew *Adam.*
[4] John 10:34.
[5] *Pepi I.*

In the *Prisse Papyrus* we have this example of the one God ideal:

> *If having been of no account, thou hast become great, and if, having been poor, thou hast become rich, when thou art governor of the city be not hardhearted on account of thy advancement, because thou hast only become the guardian of the provisions of God.*

Modern-day stewardship concepts could not have been better described. However, the important point is that there is expressed a belief in One God to whom all things belong.

In the "Maxims of Ani" we find elements of the Sermon on the Mount and the one-God theme repeated:

> *Let one give self to God. Keep thyself today for God, tomorrow will be like today. In the sanctuary of God much speaking is an abomination. Make thy prayers with a heart of love, all thy petitions offered in secret. He will perform thy affairs, he will hear what thou sayest, he will accept thine offerings. In making offerings to thy God, guard thyself against the abomination. Watch that thy eye is on His plans. Devote thyself to the adoration of his name. It is he who giveth souls to millions of forms, and he magnifieth whosoever magnifieth him.*

It is amazing how many similarities this passage has with the Sermon on the Mount. For example, the Egyptian teacher says, "Keep thyself today for God, tomorrow will be like today." In the Sermon, Jesus instructs His listeners to "not be anxious for tomorrow; for tomorrow will care for itself. Today has enough dangers of ungodliness."[6] The Egyptian teacher says, "In the sanctuary of God much speaking is an abomination. Make thy prayers with a heart of love, all thy petitions offered in secret." In the Sermon Jesus says, "When you pray, pray to your Father who is in secret, and your Father who sees in secret will respond

---

[6]Matt. 6:34.

to you. Do not use meaningless repetition, supposing that many words will cause you to be heard."[7] The Egyptian teacher says, "Watch that thy eye is on His plans." Jesus says, "Watch that thy eye be single." And in the Sermon He says, "The lamp of the body is the eye; if therefore your eye is clear, your whole body will be full of light."[8] He also warns, "Where your treasure is, there will your heart be also . . . You cannot serve God and material riches (mammon)."[9] I suppose Truth is Truth, no matter in which millennium we live and study.

In *The Egyptian Book of the Dead*, we find this description of the One Great God:

> *The holy Soul which came into being before time, the great God who liveth by unfailing order, the Whole primeval, which gave birth to the two companies of gods, through him came into being every god. One alone, he made what exists when the earth began in primeval time. Hidden of births, manifold of forms, nothing is known of his growth.*[10]

Also in the *Book of the Dead* the "self-created" God is asked, "Who then is this?" She[11] answers: "It is Ra who created names for his members and these came into being in the form of the gods who are in the following of Ra." This is a reference to the beginning of *soul-groups*, each following in or reflecting the first cause or impulse that brought them into being. Those conceived in the following of Ra are of the same soul-group and would have similar goals and perspectives on life. Those conceived in the following of Isis or Hermes or whichever godling would be of that soul-group and have similar goals and perspectives on life.

From out of the Unmanifested God came God the Creator (self-created). God the Creator conceived *cocreators*, or the

---

[7]Matt. 6:6-7.
[8]Luke 11:34.
[9]Matt. 6:21, 24.
[10]The two companies of gods are the Seraphim and Cherubim.
[11]In this section, *Nun* is the "mother" of all, self-created; therefore, I'm using the pronoun *she*.

godlings. From out of them came "the millions." The Original Great Creator then gave souls to "the millions." The plan is then very simple: Whosoever magnifies the Creator's qualities, the Creator magnifies them. It's an interrelated network of Oneness and Manyness, of Wholeness in which separateness may coexist. The ultimate goal is to subdue one's sense of separateness by magnifying the Creator's wholeness, thereby becoming one with the Whole while knowing oneself to be oneself.

As we shall see, the gods were active forces within the God.

Ra is the personification of the sun—symbolic of life, warmth, light, and day. It dispels the darkness and cold. It calls the unseen seed-life from out of the dark soil. It brings forth the light from the darkness of the night, as well as life from out of the underworld. It symbolizes the Creator's power to enliven, nourish, and enlighten. Yet, in the mystical teachings, Ra is not omnipotent, for the sun also sets. He has weaknesses, which he struggles to control. He has a personal enemy, the serpent Apep, which he struggles to subdue. He is caught in a cycle of light and darkness, day and night, consciousness and unconsciousness, life and death.

The explanation of how a god can be this great and yet have so much to struggle with goes something like this: All are gods in the higher dimensions, but they have free will and must learn to use it in harmony with the Whole. Therefore, even though the Sons and Daughters of God have powers, they are vulnerable to temptation and misdirection by choice and will. Many are also entangled in karmic laws and cycles of Nature and must free themselves from these entanglements.

The godlings crystallized their thoughts, causing them to become physically apparent or manifest. Prior to this, they were pure minds living in direct connection with the Universal Mind. Now they projected into thought-forms at first, then immersing themselves in matter with their consciousness to the point that they became *incarnate*. Since they were now acting and experiencing independently of the Creator, less conscious of the Creator and less connected to the Life Force, they began to feel alone and separated. This caused fear, and fear led to great mistakes. During these early periods on earth, some of them completely lost touch with their true celestial nature and the

Creative Forces. Others retained much or some of their connectedness. These latter ones were considered gods, yet they were also subject to the many problems and challenges that affected all who touched this realm. We will notice that throughout the ancient Egyptian teachings and records, the gods were both divine and human, powerful and vulnerable.

The word *neter* was used as we use the words *god, godly, divine,* or *divinity*. Neter literally means *renew, self-exist, self-produce*. In other words, it means *one who has the power to generate or renew life from within oneself*. This is a god. In the chapters of the ancient Egyptian text titled *Coming Forth by Day*, we find this teaching of godly renewal and self-regeneration:

> Boy god, heir of eternity, begetting and giving birth to himself.
> I am devoted in my heart more than the gods, without feigning, O thou godling.
> I have become divine.
> I have risen up in the form of a divine hawk.
> I have become pure, I have become godly, I have become conscious, I have become cocreator, I have become a soul.
> He shall be god with the gods in the Godplace.
> He shall sanctify his body completely.
> He makes godly thy soul, like the gods.
> *God divine, self-produced, primeval matter.*

Notice how similar "Boy god" is to the Judeo-Christian "Son of God," who is also the heir to eternity and begotten of God (i.e., son of God), not man (i.e, son of man). Notice also how this writer expresses *becoming* divine, sanctifying, rising up, purifying—all spiritual goals. Then notice in the second to last line how he appears to refer to a divine helper, one who helps him achieve these goals, the messiah ideal. Actually, the ancient initiate did not see this messiah outside of himself or herself. It was, in fact, the divine child growing within the individual who would ultimately be born out of one's outer physical death or, better still, one's yielding, much as a woman surrenders herself to give birth to another. This is similar to Jesus' teaching to

Nicodemus, "You must be born anew."[12]

We are physical, earthly beings, but within us is a godling, a bound angel, a sleeping beauty, seeking to be reborn, reawakened. The Edgar Cayce records speak of the part of us that *is* the angel and that this angel-self is ever before the throne of God. This godly part of us was lost during the descent but will be reborn on "the rising" or ascent.

> *Then as the guardian influence or angel is ever before the face of the Father, through same may that influence ever speak . . . Yes—through thy angel, through thy self that is the angel—does the self speak with thy Ideal!*[13]

In the phoenix principle, the death of one gives birth to the other. In Egyptian mysticism, the phoenix is a beautiful, lone bird which consumed its physical self in fire (i.e., spirit), rising renewed from the ashes to start another long life more beautiful than before. The benu bird is the physical Egyptian emblem of the great phoenix. In modern minds the benu bird would not be considered a very grand, noble bird, such as Americans would consider the eagle. But in ancient Egypt it was the very symbol of immortality, for "at the end of the inundation, recalling the primordial waters, dryness appears in the form of the first small hill, and the ash-colored heron, the benu bird, glides majestically down (seemingly from out of nowhere) and rests upon the little hill," life returns, life continues.[14]

The ancient Egyptian picture language requires us to engage our right brains in order to comprehend the meaning. We can't take these images and attempt to translate them as literal, physical pictures. If we do, we'll come up with the same concepts that many of our nineteenth-century researchers did: that is, the ancient Egyptians, for all their magnificent art, building skills (which we can only partially imitate today), and spirituality, were primitive animal worshipers with many gods. This simply is not true. The ancient images were created to convey *ideals*

---

[12]John 3:7.
[13]Cayce reading 1646-1.
[14]Pyramid texts, 1652.

associated with the creature or character of the image. Even though some of them appear bizarre, they are in fact meaning-ful and can be understood if one looks with the inner mind and a metaphorical mindset.

2

GODS AND METAPHOR

The gods of ancient Egypt are metaphors for key aspects of the origin and destiny of humanity. According to Edgar Cayce's discourses, the average citizen of ancient Egypt understood the hidden message better than we do today. Cayce further states that the characters and imagery in the Book of Revelation were also metaphors for hidden messages, and some disciples knew that and understood The Revelation better than we do today.

Here are brief insights into the hidden meaning of several key Egyptian gods.

RA, the Sun

The Sun is the source and sustainer of life, penetrator of the darkness, warmer of the cold, nurturer of the seed deep in the soil. Its rays reach out through the darkness of space and night, and give warmth, light, and life to all they touch. This is Ra (originally pronounced "ray"). Ra is the Most High God. Out of the great Ra came countless little rays, known as the sons and daughters of Ra. They are godlings from the one God, created in Its image and destined to fill all the cosmos with light and life.

HERMES, the Moon

As the rays or godlings went forth, some lost their connectedness to the great Ra. They moved too far into darkness. Their light dimmed. The darkness overcame them. Their faces turned away from the original light. All they saw were the shadows of life. They needed help. Some power needed to help them recall the original light, the original way, the original purpose. This was the power of the moon god Thoth, or Hermes in Greek. This power reflects the light to all things that have turned away from the direct light.

Hermes is most often depicted as a powerful god with an ibis head. The ibis is a bird who lives on the shore between the two worlds of the deep water and the land. The two worlds are emblems of the subconscious and conscious minds. The power to live between these two is seen as important to living the true life. Another little characteristic of the ibis is that it is one of the few birds that can eat the serpent. Again, an important metaphor for the developing godlings is to recognize the need to control their lower, self-seeking urges if they are to reunite with the creator and their original purpose.

The ancient Egyptian is not speaking of the form and function of the sun and moon in the third dimension. He or she is speaking of their meaning in dimensions of mind and spirit. In dimensions beyond the third, the sun and moon are emblems of deeper powers. For the ancient Egyptian, light is consciousness—a knowing, understanding consciousness. Darkness is unconsciousness. Living in moonlight is semiconsciousness or self-consciousness with no sense of oneness or connectedness with the source of light.

This teaching is expanded by the hidden message behind the outward passage of the sun. The rising sun represents the beginning: light dawned in the still, silent darkness—exactly as the sun rises in the morning. This dawning light penetrated the darkness and continued to its zenith, exactly as the sun rises through the morning to noon. Throughout this period all faces are turned toward the sun, receiving warmth, light, and life. The creator's power penetrates everything. Then, something changes. The created, the godlings in Ra's image, move away from the creator in order to know themselves, find themselves. The earth and the created move toward dusk. Shadows begin to fall and lengthen. The created are left to themselves. Darkness falls. Through the night souls deal with their innermost urges, while danger nips at their heels, like a little serpent. In Egyptian lore this little serpent is Apep, who nips at the heels of Ra as he traverses the underworld of night and death, seeking the horizon of resurrection and rebirth. There are many temptations, many pitfalls. But, if the godlings hold in their hearts the lightness of hope, trust, and selflessness, then they will become light of heart and, as a result, they will glide above the serpent's bite and find the new horizon. The sun will break through the night reclaiming all who are still looking, still believing.

Throughout the dark night of the souls, the moon helps remind them of the continual existence of the true light. Despite the darkness, the sun has never moved. We have moved. If one looks at the moon and intuits the source of its light, then one knows the sun still exists, the creator still exists, and one will look to the returning dawn.

ISIS AND NEPHTHYS, the two guardians

To help with this great journey into darkness, two guardians watch over each ray as it travels the earth, the underworld, and the lower heavens. In ancient Egypt, these guardians are Isis and her sister Nephthys. Isis is the power to hold the thought of the Throne of God within one's mind, whether it be only a faint memory or a vivid image. She is often depicted with the Throne of God on her head, or mind. Nephthys is the magical power to know that the unseen forces are more powerful than the seen, despite the appearance to the contrary. She is often depicted with a bowl-like receptacle on a pedestal upon her head, or mind.

These two sisters are in every death scene, at the head and

foot of the body of the deceased. They are powerful influences to help the freed soul find its way to the higher realms, higher truths. They are also seen standing behind the great god of the underworld, Osiris, whom all must pass if they are to enter the heavens. His judgment is exact; one's heart must be as light as a feather. If not, then one sinks into the underworld and cycles through the darkness to another dawn, and another opportunity to free oneself from heavy-heartedness.

ANUBIS, the sixth sense

When one has taken a long journey away from home, one can lose the trail home. If one cannot find or recall the way home, then one needs help. Anubis, the jackal-headed god, is the symbol of that help. The jackal can pick up the scent of the trail traversed to get here, and therefore the way home. At every death scene in ancient Egypt, Anubis is depicted. He is the sixth sense that recalls the way home.

OSIRIS AND SET, the two brothers' tale

In Egyptian lore two brothers were born. One loved God and cooperated lovingly with the creation. The other pursued self-seeking urges and interests and took advantage of the creation, giving little thought to the consequences of his actions and appetites. In Egypt these two brothers were Osiris and Set (sometimes called "Seth," and from which some Pharaohs took the name "Seti"). Just as in the biblical story of Cain and Abel, Set grew jealous of Osiris and killed him.

ISIS, conceiver of the messiah

One of the greatest goddesses among the hosts of godlings was Isis. She was strong, enduring, and clever. She was not to follow the weaknesses of most of her fellow gods, seeking to mingle with the sons and daughters of humankind and their carnal sensations.

Behold, Isis was in the form of a woman, skilled in words.

Her heart rebelled at the millions of men, she chose rather the millions of the gods, and she esteemed the millions of the spirits. She meditated in her heart, "Could I not be in heaven and earth like Ra, and make myself mistress of the earth and a goddess by knowing the name of the holy God?"

Isis had many adventures, but the greatest were the resurrection of Osiris, the conception and birthing of Horus, and her struggles with Set, the destroyer. The story goes like this:

Isis began as a modest divinity of the Delta (Isris). Because of her intense seeking to maintain godliness in the midst of humanness, she interacted with the great god Ra. From him she cleverly gained wisdom and power (much to his surprise). After Ra returned to the heavens, the god Osiris, her elder brother in the family of gods, chose her as his consort and she shared the throne with him. She helped him, as she had Ra, to civilize the earthly ones. She taught the art of curing disease, of growing corn, spinning flax and weaving cloth, and marrying to form a home in order to bring about some semblance of heaven in this faraway place.

When Osiris went on a great journey around the earth, she remained as regent of Egypt. She ruled so wisely and well that their younger brother Set could not take over. However, Set was full of self-seeking desires, so he cunningly convinced his older and trusting brother Osiris to lie down in a coffin, whereupon he killed Osiris, sealed the coffin, and cast it into the Nile, which carried it out to sea. It came to rest on a distant shore at the base of a tamarisk tree. The tree grew around the coffin, concealing it entirely within its trunk. When the tree was cut down by the king of that distant land, it gave off such an exquisite fragrance that its reputation spread around the world, eventually reaching Isis's ears. When she heard of this fragrant tree, she knew immediately that it was the essence of Osiris. When she arrived in that land, the queen, Astarte, entrusted her newborn son into Isis's care. Isis would have conferred immortality upon the child if the mother hadn't broken the spell by her anguished cries of terror when she saw Isis bathe the baby in purifying flames. In order to calm the mother, Isis reveals her true identity and intentions. The mother then convinces her husband, the king, to give the trunk of the magnificent tree to Isis.

Isis drew forth the coffin from the tree, and the body from the coffin. She bathed it in her tears and hid the body in the marshes. But Set found the body and cut it into fourteen pieces, scattering them far and wide. Isis, never discouraged, began a patient search for the precious fragments, finding all of them but the phallus, which had been eaten by a creature of the earth who is forever cursed for this crime.

In a magical, mystical intermingling with the reconstructed, reanimated body of Osiris, Isis conceives a child that will grow to be the true heir to the throne, contesting Set's claim to it. She then performs the first rites of embalming, restoring Osiris to eternal life, ruler of the netherworld. She is assisted in this rite by her sister Nephthys (who is also the wife of Set), her nephew Anubis (who appears in all death scenes to lead the deceased through the darkness), by Thoth, and even by the yet unborn Horus.

When Set hears of this, he captures her and imprisons her. With the help of Thoth, she conceals her pregnancy from Set and escapes. She hides Horus in the marshes, raising him in secret until he is strong enough to challenge Set (recalling the life of the baby Moses, who eventually challenges the Pharaoh).

However, she has no means of supporting herself and her baby, so she hides baby Horus among the reeds and goes begging all day. One day, returning from begging, she finds baby Horus writhing in pain and near death. Though unable to enter the marshes in his real form, Set had assumed the form of a serpent and had bitten the baby. Isis is in despair. Now, feeling all alone in this world—her father and mother dead, her husband in the netherland, her younger brother Set attacking her at every turn, and her sister Nephthys married to Set—there appears to be no one who can help her. Isis, therefore, appeals to all humankind, calling on the marsh dwellers and the fishermen, all of whom come immediately to her aid, weeping in sympathy, but powerless to help her against Set's magic. Horus, symbolizing the purity and innocence of the developing true heir, is now contaminated by the poison of the cunning, self-seeking Set. This is the poison that separates everyone who seeks self's own desires without concern for God's.

Finally, Isis calls on the Most High God to intervene on behalf of everything that is pure and true. The "Boat of Millions of Years" draws level to her and interrupts its journey for her. From out of the barque (boat) descends Thoth. After expressing surprise that her magic is not able to cleanse the child of the poison, he assures her that the power of Ra is at her disposal.

Here Isis is meeting her own karma, for it was she who long ago caused a serpent to bite Ra. Now her treasured child lies poisoned and dying before her and she needs Ra's power to cure him.

Thoth tells Isis that when the barque stopped for her and Horus, the Sun stopped and darkness came over all. The darkness will not be dispelled until the barque moves again and the Sun shines again. She and Thoth realize the significance of the Sun's stopping until Horus is cured: It means that if Horus dies, Ra's whole creation will be annihilated; and Set, the principle of evil and the consciousness of darkness, will reign forever. Isis wishes that she were Horus herself so that she would not have to see the consequences of his death. Thoth, however, declares that the magical protection enjoyed by Horus will henceforth be equal to that of the Sun. Then, in the name of the Ra, Thoth exorcises the poison from Horus's body, saying that the boat of Ra will stand still, that there will be no food, that the temples will be closed, that misery will never depart from the world, that eternal darkness will reign, that the wells will be dry, that there will be no crops and no vegetation until Horus is cured. This powerful spell of the sun-god Ra, spoken by the moon-god Thoth, conquers the poison, and Isis and all humanity rejoice. Thoth then commends the child into their care, saying that Horus is now the responsibility of all those who live on earth.

This legend repeats the recurring theme of a great and perfect creature who is misguided into activities that lead to its loss—sometimes the loss is in the form of death, sometimes in banishment, sometimes in consciousness. Then, one who loves the creature gives all of one's being to rebirth or resurrect the lost one. This often takes the form of impregnating oneself with the seed of the lost one and giving birth to its heir. The young heir to the original creation is always in danger of being poisoned, imprisoned, or misguided by the forces that brought down the original creature. It takes enduring effort to bring the heir to age in one piece. Then, the heir overthrows the deceiver and rules forever—the perfect creation again, one generation removed, and presumably wiser.

This theme can be found in stories of most cultures on the earth. It is the story of the children of God, who lost their way and must, through great effort and many trials, become heirs to their previous glory and destiny.

In this specific legend, Osiris is the original perfect one. Isis is the mind and will that resurrects him in the seed of the womb of her consciousness. Horus is the heir, always symbolized in the same manner as Ra because he represents the living manifestation of Ra (as did Osiris) and the heir to Ra's creation. Set represents the deceiver, the ego, the self-seeking aspect of every person. It destroys the perfect Osiris, wrestles with the struggling Isis (the mind and will) and poisons the growing Horus. But, enduring, Horus becomes the messiah that overcomes Set's influence, forever—with a little help from heaven (in the form of Thoth/Hermes and the boat of father Ra).

HORUS, the higher mind and messiah

Because the rays or projections of consciousness from the original consciousness have penetrated many aspects of the darkness, there needs to be a new delineation. Therefore, consciousness is identified in three levels: that which is the closest to the personal self, that which bridges the personal self to the original self, and that which is in the image of the original self, the godling, the son or daughter of Ra. We use the terms *conscious, subconscious,* and *superconscious* to identify these levels of the mind.

3

RA TA

THE STORY OF A HIGH PRIEST
BASED ON A STORY ORIGINALLY TOLD BY EDGAR CAYCE

When Nature breaks out of her rhythm, our world is often destroyed. So it had been during the Great Flood. But now the winds whispered of a return to reliable rhythms. The waters that had swallowed everything in the Great Flood stilled, waiting for the sign to withdraw from their exaggerated levels and return to tidal rhythms. Dark nights and gray days ached to find the rhythm that balances dark and light, rain and sunshine, cloud and blue sky. Then, as though heaven awoke to earth's plight, the sun broke out of the underworld and over the horizon, casting its brilliant rays into the monotony. Mingling with the lingering moisture, the sun illuminated a wondrous rainbow, bridging the grim yesterdays to hopeful, sunny tomorrows. In the light it could be seen that all had been changed. Lands that were once filled with activity and life were gone. But new lands now rose in their place.

It was time to begin anew. As the waters withdrew, they exposed little mounds of earth. Sunlight dried and warmed these silt-rich soils. It was time to live again. The great white-plumed heron descended from the heavens and finding land, alighted.

The human spirit once again moved across the little planet seeking to enter its now friendly realms, seeking to incarnate. It was time to repeople the earth. Time to plow and plant.

With the old world gone—Atlantis, Lemuria, Og, Oz, Mu— and so on—the new world emerged: Egypt, India, Persia, China, Peru, Norseland, and more.

A heavenly mind of rare power and purpose scanned the planet looking for just the right opportunity. It saw that the human remnants from the once great lands of Og, now living in and around the drying Mt. Ararat (where Noah's Ark is thought to have landed), were growing strong with a new spiritual ideal. It foresaw that these people would eventually enter Egypt and lead it on a great journey of enlightenment. This was the opportunity it was seeking. Since a prophet has little honor in his or her own tribe and land, this great mind searched for a way to come to these people from beyond their group and lands. East of Mt. Ararat, in the Persian lands, it found the tribe of Zu and a daughter whose body, heart, and mind were perfect for the incarnation of this prophet. It drew near her; with love and idealism it persuaded her deeper self to yield and, overshadowing the cells of her body, it quickened her womb, impregnating her with the seed of his form-to-be. Much to her earthly self's surprise and her father's, she found herself pregnant, though a virgin. Unfortunately, her kinspeople had little patience for her wondrous tales of inner conception and drove her from the tribe in shame. Her father, confused by his ready-to-believe-anything love for her and yet his rigid hold to physical laws, stood motionless as she was driven off.

Alone, with a mixture of confusion and expectancy, she journeyed west—not by some thought-out plan, but by some inner, intuitive urge—westward, westward! Eventually she camped near the tribe of Ararat. Ararats had no love for the tribe of Zu, so she was not welcomed, simply tolerated. But when her child was born and his beauty perceived, she was tolerated a little better. The child grew in stature and wisdom, revealing a "knowing" that quickly identified him as a prophet. In one of the child's presentations, he prophesied the entrance of this tribe into the rich lands of Egypt, conquering it and beginning an era of enlightenment that would not be rivaled in the history of humankind. King Ararat, moved deeply by this prophecy, began to hold the boy in high esteem, giving comfort and support to him and his mother—whose life had finally taken a turn for the better.

The boy was of unusual coloring. His skin was lighter than his mother's, his hair was like the sun. Because of these features he was called Ra Ta, "Sun in Earth."

Ra Ta showed a remarkable ability to control wild animals, particularly the great cats. He would attract them to himself and then direct their activities. At the age of twenty-one, he led King Ararat and his families down out of the mountains, across the plains, and into the wealthy lands of Egypt. Some nine hundred souls composed this invasion force. Lions, under the control of young Ra Ta, led the way. The natives of Egypt were amazed by the sight of this sunlit boy and his lions, leading a large band of hardy, life-struggling mountain people into their land of ease and plenty. It was cal!ouses versus manicures, skins versus silks, muscle versus tender flesh. In other words, it was no contest.

In a quickly held meeting of the native rulers, a young Egyptian scribe proposed that they welcome these newcomers rather than fight them. There was plenty in Egypt for all to live well together, and it appeared that the conquerors were capable of taking Egypt if forced to. It was agreed. The proposal was carried to the invaders. Some Ararats laughed at the idea, others were inspired by the spirit of cooperation and coexistence. Ra Ta was among the more cooperative minds, and so it was agreed. However, even though there would be co-rulership over the lands, the Ararats would choose who among the natives would be the co-ruler. The sting of this counterproposal never left the young scribe who had proposed coexistence, but he was resigned to fate. Little did he know that the conquerors would choose him to be the co-ruler—a decision that would raise him from the respectable status of a teaching scribe to the exalted position of co-ruler and councilor on the governing body of all of Egypt during its greatest period of enlightenment.

Why did Ra Ta and the Ararats want Egypt? It was not simply for the easier life that could be lived there. The great mind that scanned the earth for opportunity had determined that, on this particular planet, the center of the universal activities of nature, as well as spiritual forces, was in Egypt. The longitude and latitude lines that pass over the greatest mass of the earth cross at Giza. It was also a location that would have the least amount of disturbance from the convulsive earthquakes that continued after the destruction of Lemuria and Atlantis, as well as the lingering effects of the Great Flood. Egypt was the place to continue not only the physical evolution, but the spiritual evolution as well. The willingness of the Ararats and the native Egyptians to be led in the direction of spiritual development and enlightenment made these the right peoples and the best lands to begin the new era. Therefore, the prophet came to them.

However, many challenges to this great ideal would beset Ra Ta and these seeking peoples, challenges that would test them to the limits of their understanding and patience.

First was the challenge of coexistence. It would be a marriage of two very different peoples. After a period of dissension among many of the young native leaders of Egypt, peaceful arrangements for coexistence were finally reached. As an act of peace and cooperation, the name of the young native leader chosen to co-rule was changed to Aarat, in line with the house of Arart (of which the invading King Ararat was a descendant). The co-ruler position and title gave the young Egyptian scribe recognition among his fellow natives, while the new name gave him recognition among the young leaders in the tribe of Ararat.

Aging King Ararat began to withdraw from the daily rulership role, preferring to focus his time on organizational matters. He turned over much of the rulership to his son Araaraart. (A mouthful for the modern tongue, but that was his name. The sleeping Cayce pronounced it "Raaaa-art." For our purposes here, I'll refer to him from here on as *Art*.) Art was thirty years old when his father turned over the kingship to him.

Ra Ta and Art were strongly inclined to a ruling council that would cooperate with them and had some sense of their goals of spiritual development and enlightenment. So they began to choose council members according to their ideals. Those with ideals that were in accord with the great plan were prime candidates. This caused much turmoil among the upper-class Egyptians who had expected to be put on the governing council, regional councils, and other posts simply because of their status, not their ideals. The native co-ruler, now called Aarat, was actually more attuned with the ideals and plans of Art and Ra Ta than with his own upper class. He was also enamored with one of the invading tribe's young ladies, which made him even more inclined to their ways of thinking! The young lady taught him much about the history and customs of the Ararat.

King Art gathered many about him to act as a governing council. The highest council was the Inner Council, which ruled the general circumstances of the people as a whole. This council included some priests from Ra Ta's team of spiritual teachers, trainers, and initiates, some native leaders, some leaders from the tribe of Ararat, and, of course, the king himself. Later, when a remnant of Atlanteans landed on their shores unexpectedly, the Inner Council also included some of their leadership—among them the great Axtel, known to most of us as the legendary Ajax.

Ajax and his Atlantean peoples added another complication to the mix of minds and wills involved in this emerging country. Atlanteans were very different from most people on the earth. The only similarity they had with the native Egyptians was plenty of experience with leisure living. But the Egyptians enjoyed their leisure living from the bounty of Nature's resources in their land, whereas the Atlanteans used the powers of the imaginative forces to bring about their leisure living, making thought-forms and "things" to do the labor necessary for leisure existence. The Egyptians enjoyed the gifts of Nature; the Atlanteans took hold of Nature and the Creative Forces and made life leisurely!

As far as the tribe of Ararat and the tribe of Ajax are concerned, their only point of mutual understanding was their common history and customs from the land of Og. However, their purposes for life and their concepts of other peoples were nearly opposite. Atlanteans, though humbled by the destruction of their great culture and continent, were a powerfully dominating people. Weakness or timidity in others was seen as a subordinating characteristic, and such peoples were enslaved or used by the Atlanteans. Nevertheless, the Atlanteans knew the forces of Nature and the Creative Forces intimately. They knew how to use them. Ra Ta and Art had to get these power people to catch their vision of a new era of enlightenment for all peoples, and then they could enjoy the power these strange ones brought to the Inner Council and the lands of Egypt.

Beyond the Inner Council was another that focused on the supervision of the many departments of government, similar to the U.S. president's cabinet, for the governmental departments were much as they are today. According to the Cayce readings, there is nothing in the present that hasn't existed from the beginning; only the form or manner of its use has changed. However, the art of governing has been lost and is only recently being rediscovered. According to the Cayce material, in ancient Egypt order, systems, organization, resource management, evaluation of talent, training, enhancing talent, and so on were common knowledge of the most illiterate of these people. It was an art that blended a higher level of consciousness with an understanding of the physical laws of Nature. As Nature organized and utilized her forces and resources, so these people organized and utilized their forces and resources.

With the councils established, King Art began opening mines in Ophir, later known as Kadesh, now called Persia. He also opened mines in the land now known as Abysinnia (Ethiopia), and those lands yet to be discovered in upper Egypt. From these and other mines, he gathered rich minerals of gold, silver, iron, lead, zinc, copper, tin; and precious stones—onyx, beryl, sardis, diamond, amethyst, and opal. From the seas near what is now called Madagascar, he gathered pearls. As mining boomed, stonecutters began developing their skills and gathering the materials necessary to build the grand residences of the king's people and the temples of the priests' followers.

All the women of the clan or tribe were housed for the evening in large buildings connected with the temples. The men were housed in large buildings connected with the king's palaces. The buildings were beautifully structured in tiered layers. Each hall had three to four tiered floors. The private sleeping rooms were small, seven feet by nine feet, with eight- to ten-foot ceilings. All items, such as blankets, rugs, linens, etc., were handmade. These tiered halls of private rooms connected to great chamber halls for group gatherings dealing with learning and recreation, such as dancing. There were special halls and chambers for conceiving, birthing, and raising children. There were also special halls and chambers for initiations and sacred teachings. According to Cayce, the buildings were designed and built to demonstrate the "relationships of individuals to individuals, and relationships of individuals as individuals . . . to the Creative Forces [personal attunement]" and of "masses" of individuals "to the Creative Forces [group gatherings and attunement]."[1]

Ra Ta's priests and temples and King Art's councils and palaces began the first cooperative separation of church and state. As Art had gathered about him those with whom he felt he could govern and reach the goals to which he aspired, so Ra Ta gathered about himself those whom he discerned were right for his goals. These were quite different from the king's requirements. Ra Ta sought those who would harken to his ideas about unseen worlds beyond this one and areas within the body that represented the nonphysical life and the activities that occurred during the intermission between one incarnation and another, between one day's activity and the night's sleep activity! He was teaching that this inner life was important and worth knowing. The natives held more strongly to the material outer life and the enjoyment of it, rather than seeking some unseen inner life. The Egypt that Ra Ta entered was a highly developed material civilization. He brought a new view, one difficult to comprehend from a strictly material perspective. Nevertheless, the people remembered how, as a young man, he had led the lions into Egypt, so they listened to him. He also uncovered archaeological evidence to support his intuitive teachings about their prehistory. This caused many to come to him and listen. Some of these even committed themselves to the rigors of his temples.

In the temples, exercises for increasing spiritual awareness and attunement to the Universal Forces were developed, taught, and practiced. Stages of initiation and enlightenment were designed. Aspiring priests and priestesses proceeded to advance through these body-changing, mind-changing stages. The first

---

[1]Cayce reading 294-149.

stages were in the Temple of Sacrifice, where cleansings and purifications were the focus, mostly relating to perfecting the body. The second stages were in the Temple Beautiful, where attunement and enlightenment were the focus, mostly relating to the mind and spirit.

The altars were prepared according to inner guidance. They included sacrificial altars and beautification altars. They did not sacrifice animals, birds, beasts, reptiles, or humans on these altars, as some today may think. Upon these altars individuals put their faults and blotted them out with the fires of the unseen forces that were set in motion by attunement to the powers of the Spirit. When these cleansings were combined with the inner guidance to commit oneself to a specific career of service, one could then make great leaps forward in freedom from earthiness and limited consciousness. This was only done after the seekers had chosen to give themselves to these services. None was forced into the temples, and once in the temples none was forced to progress through the various stages. Each had to choose or be moved from within himself or herself.

The Temple of Sacrifice was built for those who sought physical and mental cleansing. To compare this facility to something today, we'd have to combine one of our best hospitals with one of our best health spas. Restructuring and cleansing the body could employ several means, from surgeries to scented baths, from chemistry to massage, from painful changes to nirvanic transformation.

The Temple of Beauty (or Temple Beautiful) was built for those who sought to consecrate and dedicate themselves to attunement and service. To compare this facility to something today, we'd have to combine one of our highly idealistic universities with one of our most loving missionary-type religious organizations, and further combine them with one of our prayer and meditation centers. This is not something we would easily do today. The Temple Beautiful was amazingly expanding for its participants. It combined body, mind, and soul development with service to God, to humans, and to the world. The program was not reclusive nor elitist. Whether one was channeled to work in the sacred services of the altars or in the daily labors of the granary, both were seen equally as divinely manifesting their ultimate potential to magnify God in life.

In these ancient temples and times, the body was worshiped much more than it is today; it was worshiped as divine in itself. It was considered the temple of the living God. Beauty was divine. Symmetry, proportion, and radiance were considered to be of divine inheritance. Beauty was next to godliness. Therefore, the Temple of Sacrifice, as a combination of hospital and spa, was a busy place for transformation toward godliness. As bodies were more perfectly structured and purer in function, participants would then enter the Temple Beautiful to concentrate and consecrate their bodies, their lives, their activities in attunement and service. According to the Cayce readings, the purpose for all of this was: that there might be a closer relationship of individuals to the Creator, and a better relationship of individuals with one another.

Many of those who advanced in these temples became staff members of the temples, cleansing and guiding others. Some became artisans, politicians, business people, all with high ideals and standards. Some became directors and staff members of smaller temples throughout the many regions of Egypt. Some became ambassadors to temples in other countries. Ra Ta became high priest of the main temples in Egypt as well as a traveler to other countries, as teacher and colleague with other spiritual leaders. There was only one language on the earth at this time, so it was easy to communicate anywhere in the world.

Though much had been lost by the Great Flood, there was a regular exchange of ideas with other lands, such as Poseidia (remnant island of the great continent of Atlantis) and Og, the Pyrenees in present-day Spain, and Sicily, even with those countries we know today as Norway, China, India, Peru (a remnant of Lemuria), and America. Though these were not their names at that time, they were the locations where tribes gathered to repeople the earth.

Despite many gains, Ra Ta struggled with disappointment and discouragement. He was in a constant wrestling match with earthly ideals held by a number of the people. Many were into the comforts of living only the material life well. Some of these were also into controlling people as subordinates and slaves for their own benefit, an action which did not fit with Ra Ta's ideal of one God and one family of the children of God, all equal siblings. Also in these early periods, many of the people were contaminated with animalistic influences, leaving them virtually unable to conceive of spiritual realms and realities and requiring much hard work to cleanse them of these influences. Changes were necessary if the spiritual ideals and understandings were to be realized.

The Cayce readings state that we are coming to a period of time that is exactly like this ancient period in Egypt—a return in the cycle of things. According to Cayce and other sources, it will begin as it did then. First, there will be the cleansing of the earth, not by water this time but by fire, or something akin to fire. Some think this was the atomic/nuclear bomb war that was expected but hasn't manifested. Perhaps we are beyond that. Some believe it may be by solar radiation due to the dissipation of the ozone-protective layer. Some say that the Van Allen belts will break down during a magnetic pole shift, allowing solar and space radiation to directly hit the surface of our planet. There are many ideas about this. As before, this cleansing will be followed by a struggle to set the new ideals higher than the old ones. We will be wrestling with the very same issues as Ra Ta and his band of seekers. This will be followed by a great era of wondrous beauty, enlightenment, and creativity, as was seen in ancient Egypt's four to ten thousand years of glory.

The length of Egypt's glory period depends on who's doing the counting and the method of counting. Cayce dates this post-Great-Flood renaissance beginning as early as 11,016 B.C. in reading 341-9. His readings seem to be dating the coming new period of change as beginning as early as 1998 to as late as 2001, and in full swing by 2038. However, it is unclear exactly what will be beginning. But it is clearly stated that it will follow the pattern of experiences, activities, and opportunities that were set in ancient Egypt. These include a transition to a new body type, which he calls the fifth root race. It'll also include a new view of death, less fear of this transition than we have today, and more conscious understanding of what actually happens to us during and after this thing called death.

So, the priest or seer Ra Ta had a very busy life in ancient Egypt. Still, he devoted much time to keeping himself in communion with those Creative Forces that brought knowledge and guidance to him. He also stayed informed of the spiritual progress made in other lands. From time to time, he would visit other lands to meet their leaders and review their practices, as well as share his views and customs.

As often happens among highly motivated people, cooperative efforts are rarely without some turmoil. During his absences, there arose a growing dissension among the people, both in the temples and the palaces. Some were beginning to claim that Ra Ta was leaving too much to his subordinates; the native councilors especially found such fault with him. Others who had allowed avarice to arise in their hearts and minds began to covet control of the wealth of this great land, especially the wealth of its temples. These contentious voices generated increasing questioning and doubts about Ra Ta and his beliefs and practices. Gradually, some began to misuse their offices and influence to gratify their personal interests and desires. The special knowledge that had been shared with many of the priests, such as how to use chemical, aromatic, and vibrational stimuli to aid the body in cleansing itself of the powerful forces of earth-life, was being used by some to actually stimulate the bodies to baser urges. Some of these entrusted people began to brew drinks and create incenses and rhythms that caused the fires of the body and mind to go against everything that had been perfected in the temple work, kindling physical fires rather than spiritual ones.

Ra Ta remained unaware of this growing dissension and subversion until, returning from one of his journeys, he accidentally walked in on one of these stimulation sessions. As he observed the activity and perceived the ingredients and intentions of stimulants, he realized that they were for the aggrandizing of the lusts of the body rather than the cleansing of animalistic influences that the sacrificial priests were supposed to be doing. For Ra Ta, the blatant arrogance and disobedience of the sacrificial priests were the most shocking elements of this discovery. There arose a mighty turmoil in the temples. People losing their positions. People claiming they had nothing to do with it, while others claimed they did. Those outside of the temples began to want Ra Ta to explain what he had been doing that let the situation get so bad. An official inquiry began. Greater and greater stress was laid upon the high priest and his supporters. Those who wanted him ousted began to look for ways to bring him down and out of power. Factions arose— small groups of people working in common against the main temple group led by Ra Ta. Even in the king's councils, a group opposed to Ra Ta began to plan ways to undercut his influence. One plan proved effective.

Among the daughters of the temple priests was one who was the king's favorite. Her name was Isris. She was beautiful, creative, and cheerful. Her music, dance, and song were often performed before the king, the council, and visitors from other lands. Those who wanted to dislodge Ra Ta and reduce his influence in the temples induced this beautiful daughter to gain the high priest's favor and show him her beauty and talent. Isris agreed, but not out of her own volition. These factious councilors were persecuting her clan, and she acted in order to release her people from this persecution in return for her support.

As she appeared before the high priest with all her magic, the schemers watched Ra Ta's eyes for the telltale signs of weakness. Instead, they found that Ra Ta was more filled with joy at the daughter's beauty and talent than with lust to possess her. Sexually joining with this daughter would have been a violation of the laws, both the physical law of the land and the spiritual law which Ra Ta himself had taught. But it wasn't the law that dissuaded Ra Ta from possessing her; he simply had no lust in him. Instead, he gloried in his success at helping to develop such a wonderful human being in the temples.

It appeared that the plan had failed. But there was one thing Ra Ta sought more than anything else: pure bodies through which souls could incarnate more divinely. In the Temple of Sacrifice, these pure bodies were achieved through a painstakingly long, slow process of cleansing and sanctifying. When we desire something enough, it can be made to look right no matter by what means it is gained. The schemers began to encourage Ra Ta to consider pairing perfect couples in a special breeding program in order to more easily and rapidly produce perfect bodies. A breeding program was what was needed to fulfill Ra Ta's greatest desire. Since Ra Ta had one of the most perfect male bodies in all of Egypt, he should certainly play a key part in this righteous breeding program. Also, of course, since Isris had one of the most perfect female bodies in all of Egypt, she should certainly play a key part in this plan. In fact, it would make the most sense to pair the two best bodies to one another, wouldn't it? Thus, despite all the laws to the contrary, this seemingly high-purposed plan hooked Ra Ta completely. Of course, when one is doing something that others may have a difficult time fully appreciating, it is best to do it in secret. So, Ra Ta and his little band of priests and priestesses quietly began their righteous breeding program, without consulting the ruling council.

Marital relationships as we know them today did not exist then. Two people did not take vows and join together to form a home and create a family to which they were bound by blood and devotion. Companions were appointed by the leaders with the ultimate purpose being to serve the needs of the state as a whole. The individuals' desires and opinions did not matter in these decisions. Mating was not for life, and the children were raised separately.

In the temples, these rules and practices were even more guarded and restrictive. There was a specific Temple of Creation set aside for these purposes. Many individuals were required to supervise these activities, carefully holding everyone to the rules. Children born to selected companions were taken from them after three months of age and raised by groups in other halls. Then, as they reached certain ages, they would move to other select halls. As a young person began to show certain skills or interests, he or she would be guided to those specialties.

In his travels, Ra Ta had observed other ways to raise a people. Combining some of these ideas with his own inner guidance, he began to design and encourage arrangements and facilities that linked the male and female parents with the offspring in a special area set aside for them (a sort of "home room" idea). Though the child would still spend much time in the group training halls, he or she would always return to the "home room" and to the parents. Ra Ta, in cooperation with the ruling council, had set a law that companions remain loyal to their unit. However, couples still did not choose one another but were selected by the leadership. Also, more than one female was allowed in a family unit. Even so, Isris was not a part of Ra Ta's long-established family unit and their mating had not been approved by the council. Therefore, in accordance with the agreed-upon law, Ra Ta should not mate with her—and he had helped to set this law! But all this was lost in the headiness of the great goal of perfect bodies for high, spiritual purposes.

Now, as many of us have learned (often the hard way), we may very well conceive something in secret, we may even grow something in secret, but eventually, despite all of our efforts to the contrary, it will make its presence known to the rest of the world. When the issue of Ra Ta's and Isris's righteous liaison was born, perfect in every way, it was a stunning shock to the king and the ruling council. Half brokenhearted, half confused, the king could not believe that his favorite had somehow become sexually involved with the high priest's operations—intimate operations. The schemers had Ra Ta right where they wanted him. They simply counseled the king that the laws that Ra Ta himself had taught were broken for the mere pleasure of having the most beautiful woman in all of Egypt, who also happened to be the king's favorite. With the council's support and many of the temple priests' support, the king held a hearing on this matter, found them guilty of breaking the law, and banished them all from Egypt, forever. Furthermore, there was no way the king was going to let them go off with their new little love nest, so he took their perfect child from them and assigned her to one of the infant-raising groups.

Ra Ta was dismayed. How had his high ideals become so confused and mingled with the base desires and petty politics of this world? Where had he gone wrong? How could he have been so naive, so gullible, so blindly trusting of his advisors? All he wanted now was to regain something of the vision and wisdom that had originally guided him.

Isris was also dismayed. How had she gone from the simple purpose of freeing her clan from persecution to this high crime that resulted in banishment from her people and the king who so enjoyed her? Where did it all go wrong? What would become of her now? Not to mention the emptiness she felt from the loss of her baby, her first baby, whom she would never hold again.

It was a sad, somber caravan that journeyed out of the bounty of Egypt and into the strange lands of Nubia—some 230 souls plus the weary high priest—high priest of little more than sand and scorpions.

The hot, dry Nubian hills were honeycombed with cool caves. Ra Ta's little band settled into these caves and organized their resources, for it was expected to be a very long stay. In these reclusive shelters, the high priest withdrew from the activities of the busy world, slipping regularly into the deeper meditations on the Universal Consciousness. Not since his early days had he so much time for meditation, attunement, channeling, and recording. It wasn't long before he regained his "sight" and began to crystallize his powers beyond anything he had previously manifested. Now he could bring the Creative Forces to bear on the demands of physical life. Things began to get much better for this little band of seekers—and for the native Nubians, who quickly realized that this stranger was in good stead with Nature. The Cayce readings explain that as Ra Ta entered more and more into closer and closer relationships with the Creative Forces, greater were the abilities for him to bring about material manifestations of his growing spiritual relationship. Nature began to cooperate with him and the needs of his people and those associated with them. The readings also tell of his cosmic attunement, in which he began to receive guidance and understanding about the universe, the solar system, and this planet. He began to publish reckonings of the cycles of the moon, the magnetic poles of the earth, longitude and latitude of the planet, its relations to other planets and constellations—using no equipment, the information coming from inner attunement! The readings state that as his attunements got closer and closer to the Universal Consciousness, the Sun god in him awakened. Ra was born. His name would forever be associated with the early wisdom of this culture and time.

The same had happened for Isris. In her association with the priest, his teachings, and practices, she had gained a closer relationship with the great Universal Consciousness and, as a result, Isis—the greatest goddess of Egyptian mythology and legend—was awakening within her soul and mind. She would eventually become the leader of Egypt's seekers in Ra's stead.

Rumors of these great events spread back to Egypt, reaching

the ears of a now troubled Inner Council. Things were not going well in the land of plenty. The centralizing ideal that Ra Ta embodied was lost, scattering the energies of the people. Self-interest groups were everywhere. Armed rebellions against King Art's leadership broke out, something that was never a likelihood during the joint leadership with Ra Ta. Every form of success that happened in Nubia seemed to point to the fact that Egypt had acted in haste. More and more people from the various factions sought audiences with the king to call for the return of Ra Ta before everything was completely out of control. Despite these overtures, the obstacles to Ra Ta's return seemed insurmountable. King Art would literally have to reverse his ruling, change the charges against them and the sentence of banishment, while at the same time placate those who oversaw the downfall of the priest and had subsequently gained much power in the land. Nevertheless, anarchy was not a pleasant option for even these, and Ibex's rebellion had nearly broken the country in two. In the temples, those who had advanced in their purification and attunement were hearing and reading about Ra Ta advancements, and they wanted to study with him again. The Atlanteans also had grown weary of the level of life in Egypt and wanted that cosmically connected priest to rejoin the council.

The three main peoples of Egypt—natives, Ararats, and Atlanteans—had come to think of themselves as the elect, the chosen on the earth. Now, through distractions, confusing events, and decisions, they recognized that envy, selfishness, strife, contention, and the lusts of the things of the body and the material world had separated them from their calling and vision. The mood throughout Egypt was changing. The priest must return.

As a result of this situation, secret go-betweens were contracted to begin discussions with Ra Ta concerning his return to the position of high priest of Egypt. The pull back into the strife of politics, meetings, negotiations, and the general high activity of material life caused Ra Ta to age very quickly, consuming his life force in ways that were not good, pulling him away from his attunement. Yet, he knew that ultimately his return to spiritual leadership in Egypt was his destiny. So he and his band began the long trek back to the land of plenty and the Temples of Sacrifice and Beauty. Many of the emissaries to the various councils thought that he was not going to make it. He physically looked decrepit and near death. But he survived and arrived amid a great fanfare of welcomers and well-wishers.

Upon arriving at the temples, Ra Ta again withdrew himself from daily contact with the people and the business of material life, choosing to reattune himself to the Creative Forces. In doing such, he caught sight of a great vision and purpose that lay before him: to build a facility that would initiate thousands into the deeper truths and would remain on the earth as a monument to the unseen life, the unseen powers of the Spirit, and would also serve as a chronogram for those who knew how to use it. This was the next major focus of Ra Ta's work, the conceiving, designing, and building of the Great Pyramid of Giza.

But first, the old man had to become young again, strong enough to handle this great task that would take one hundred years to complete. Ra Ta began to rejuvenate his body. Through a series of exercises, cleansing processes, dietary changes, and special attunement sessions, he took hold of the Creative Forces and let go of the aging influences, rejuvenating himself to the beauty, strength, and clarity of a young man. It took him seven years—one complete cycle for the human body to renew all of its cells.

When the rejuvenated high priest came out from the temples to marshal the resources necessary for his great project, the world was stunned by his appearance. Word of his rejuvenation spread throughout Egypt, Nubia, and the world. People journeyed from faraway places to see the priest who once visited them and who was now rejuvenated. But the old Ra Ta was not what they found. The Sun god Ra stood in Egypt's place of power, sole leader of the country, eclipsing even the king's power. Ra was considered the greatest example of the benefits of his teachings, and all listened to him.

United again, Egypt began to prosper. One ideal, one purpose, one leader, one people created the first truly national mass society with icons, themes, and slogans, merging all differences into one, cohesive body: Egypt in the Golden Sun. The energy rose to high levels of achievement in every corner of life. Egypt

was the center of the world, and the Great Pyramid was to become the central temple.

While in his attunement in Nubia, Ra Ta reached a level of
consciousness that enabled him to develop a relationship with
one who would become an equally great god of ancient Egypt,
the later Greeks would call him Hermes Trismegistus, but the
Egyptians called him Thoth. Thoth brought to Ra Ta the sacred
geometry necessary to design the Pyramid so that it would not
only stand for thousands of years, but would secretly carry
within it the mysteries of life. Together, Thoth and Ra designed
and built the Pyramid and initiated thousands of seekers.

Isis, too, played an increasingly greater role in the enlightenment of Egypt. Her presence and "knowing" had a major influence on these peoples, causing them to have a unique
attitude toward women. Now, not only did a woman become
that influence upon which humanity depended for incarnation
(physical birth), nourishment, and comfort, but for spiritual
development as well. Isis's position was equal to the king's, and
many sought her aid in understanding the goals and teachings
of Ra.

Then came the period when all the monuments and the Great
Pyramid were completed. The ideals were clearly established.
The records preserved. And the work needed to be carried on by
others growing in their "knowing." Ra, having finished his work,
ascended again in the mount, and was borne away. However,
the ascension of Ra Ta from earthly incarnation did not affect
the power and influence of the spirit of Ra, which lives on even
today. In reading 294-151 it is prophesied that he will return: "Is
it not fitting, then, that these [Ra Ta's little band of exiles] must
return? as this priest [Ra, now Edgar Cayce] may develop himself to be in that position, to be in the capacity of a *liberator* of
the world in its relationships to individuals in those periods to
come; for he must enter again at that period, or in 1998."

4

IMAGES AND MEANINGS

Some of the profound Egyptian teachings are in picture stories. An Egyptian initiate in the secret teachings would have known the deeper meanings conveyed in these pictures. Common themes were creation, transformation, great journeys, and death, especially the post-death journey.

The Creation Picture

Illustration 17 is a creation picture story. Despite its rich content, with insights into the creation and destiny of life, the picture's message can be missed by someone not schooled in the basics of mystical knowledge. For instance, when the picture is read from top to bottom, we see that out of the crown chakra of a circular woman representing Mother God, a child is conceived in the Mother's image. The child stretches forth its arms in a gesture acknowledging the pure, all-inclusive circle, which represents God and God-consciousness. The ultimate circle for the ancient Egyptian is the Sun. It is the Ra (pronounced "ray") from which all of Ra's children come, the rays from the great Ray.

Also in the picture is a dung beetle, whose earthly practice is to roll its dross in a ball toward the morning Sun. As the Sun wakes the dark and still earth from the night with its life-giving light and warmth, the beetle plants its seed into its dung ball, from which new life ultimately emerges. To the ancient Egyptian, this ugly little creature's conception ritual represented a great teaching: Our birth was originally in the heavens or dimensions above this one, in the image of God, to be God's companions, but we have descended from heaven and God-consciousness into the dung of life in a lower dimension. Yet even here on earth we can plant the seed of our resurrection, rejoining the circle of God and God-consciousness.

Below the beetle stand the goddesses Isis and Nephthys, sisters representing conception and magic, respectively. They assist this rebirth while traveling on the barque (boat) of the gods, which itself is heading always toward the circle of God, as indicated by the circle to the right and at the bow of the barque.

The upside-downness of this world is shown in the upside-down cobra and the Mother God's upside-down relation to the earth. Below the barque, the mother of creation (Nut) safely holds the barque in the waters of time and space. The many people in the boat represent the many experiences that a soul has on this great journey.

The large, raised serpent on the left side of this picture represents the raising of the life force of physical life, the kundalini energy of Hinduism, to a level at which it can reconnect with its heavenly origins and their higher vibes.

The Descent and Ascent of Heaven

Illustrations 18 and 19 are from the tomb walls of Ramses. Here we have one of the most amazing mystical concepts to come out of ancient Egypt. I have provided the actual color image of the wall (18), then selected out the specific part on which we want to focus (19). It is viewed from right to left.

The two large lions represent Yesterday (on the right) and To-morrow (on the left). The story begins with the descent of the heavenly barque (boat) from out of the heavens. Two souls (symbolized by the two birds with human heads; more on this in chapter 7) are giving homage to a symbol which has the body of a beetle and the head of a ram, representing the beginning period (ram-headed Aries) of entry into material and material-ism (the dung beetle). On the bow of the barque sits a monkey, indicating that the souls incarnated first in physical forms used by the monkey, as Darwin so accurately observed. Looking across to the lion of Tomorrow, you will see that the barque of heaven is rising out of the Earth realms back to the heavens with a bird on its bow, indicating that we will fly above this plane in forms as light as a small bird. Notice how two human-headed cobras are helping to pull the barque out of the material plane, indicating the importance of the kundalini energy within the body in order to achieve this ascent to heaven again. Why two? In ancient mystical teachings the kundalini is composed of three parts. One is the central portion, called the susumna, and correlates to the spinal cord and the cerebrospinal system. The other two weave around the central one in a double-helix spi-ral, called ida and pegalli, and correlate to the woven nerves of the autonomic nervous system, with its close control over the lungs and endocrine glands, which are the breath of life and the seven spiritual chakras, respectively.

In the lower central portion of this image we see two hands holding up or honoring the sun disk of Ra. The two hands are the image of the ka, the spirit, and in this case they are the Great Spirit. The solar disk is the Great Consciousness. The three be-ings to the right and left of the hands and disk are the personali-ties of the past and the future that each soul will experience. In our souls' early experiences in this dimension, we will be look-ing back toward the creation and the fall, but as we focus on what has to be done in this realm, then we begin to look forward toward the resurrection and ascension.

The fourth figure on each side is our priestly higher selves. This aspect of our consciousness will and can guide us through this descent and ascent. Notice how the first priest is smaller and girdled about the waist, whereas the second is large and without restriction around his middle. This reflects our level of spiritual attunement at these two points of transition (small and large) and the influence of our lower urges during the descent (the belt around the waist).

Notice how the rudders of the descending barque are large and those of the ascending one are small. This reflects the truth that our willfulness steered us into this mess (large rudders), but that our willingness to be led (small rudders) by the higher forces (the human-headed cobras, raised kundalini consciousness and energy) will steer us out of here.

The Great Death Scenes

Without a doubt, the ancient Egyptians were obsessed with the mystery of death. *The Egyptian Book of the Dead* reads as a death manual and was intended to guide the deceased one's soul through the many transitions and realms beyond this one.

In the following illustrations, you'll notice that death was not known as an end of the person, but simply an important transition, from out of which individuals could and probably would return! To the ancient initiate, there was no ultimate death.

We can see this in illustration 49. The deceased is coming out of the coffin with the symbols of life (the ankh) in both hands! The deceased lives! The four children of Horus represent the same elements or transitions that Ezekiel and John saw, in their respective revelations, as the four beasts. These forces must become subservient to the higher self if the soul is to resurrect—as it appears that our friend in the picture has done.

In illustration 50, we see the ba (soul) coming out of the mummified body. Notice that the ankh which the soul holds has no descender on it; this is because this soul is no longer incarnate.

In illustration 51, we see the guide of the dead, Anubis, assisting the separation of the soul from the preserved body. In ancient Egypt, it was believed that no one could enter the next world unless one's earthly body was preserved from decay after death. If a person's body was allowed to disintegrate, that spirit (ka) would be doomed to wander as a lonely ghost. The Cayce readings recommend that all bodies be cremated to fully dispose of them and to release the soul/spirit from any attachment.

However, the readings also recommend that we all work toward resurrecting our bodies, ascending into heaven with them! He says that death is the last initiation/test to be overcome.

Attunement and Passage Through the Two Gates

In illustration 13, we see the three-times great Thoth, or Hermes, holding his two staffs, showing the raised kundalini energies of the lower self and the upper self. In his other hand, he is giving life to the attuned initiate. This initiate is holding the symbols of the shepherd's crook, the kundalini pathways, and the flail, symbol of control over one's emotions and senses. Below the initiate's elbow, you'll notice the disk of the Unseen One, around which is the serpent with the ankh. Next to this, you'll see Horus, in the form of the hawk, wearing the hats of the ruler of the upper and lower worlds. Next to Horus is the staff upon which is the feathered companion to Hermes, Maat, symbolizing truth. In the middle of the picture are blooming lotuses.

Illustration 52 shows the two gates. First, our seeker is encouraging his or her soul to the higher worlds by entering the lower gate (which Cayce identifies with the lyden center, second chakra). Then we see the soul at the entrance to the upper gate (which Cayce identifies with the pineal center, crown chakra). In illustration 53 we see again the two gates. The lower is busy with detail, but the upper is clear and pure, with the all-seeing eye over it. In this image, our seeker is being tested in the balance by Maat (symbolizing truth) to see if he or she is worthy of the return journey to heaven and transformation into the angelic being he or she originally was and will be again.

5

TEMPLES AND BODIES

I n mysticism, the human body is the temple of the living God. It is the abode of the soul and spirit. Therefore, temples for worshiping God and initiating spiritual seekers were laid out in a manner to reflect this truth. The human body has three major chambers: (1) the abdominal cavity, (2) the pulmonary cavity, and (3) the cranial cavity. Most ancient temples also have three major chambers: a courtyard, a pillared hall, and a sanctuary. In most temples these three chambers rise as one moves through the temple, from the lower courtyard to the highest part of the temple, the sanctuary. The court is often open and large, as the abdomen, and is where seekers are to eliminate their selfish interests and urges. The next chamber is the hypostyle hall with many pillars or pylons, reflecting the ribs in the pulmonary cavity. After the hypostyle there is usually a narrow passage to the sanctuary, reflecting the body's narrow neck passage to the head. The courtyard, pillared hall, and sanctuary of an ancient temple represent the abdomen, chest, and head of the body, the true temple.

Why three? Mystically, three represents the three levels of consciousness (conscious, subconscious, and superconscious) and the three dimensions of life (physical, mental, and spiritual).

The courtyard is for cleansing and eliminating selfish thoughts and urges, the hypostyle hall is for lifting the thoughts to the higher ideals, and the narrow passage leading to the sanctuary is for the selectivity required by measuring the heart and intent of the seeker. Often temple sanctuaries are divided into two parts: the holy place and the holy of holies. The holy place is for preparation and sanctification before entering into the presence of God, and the holy of holies is where God meets the seeker. This is the way in the ancient temple and the human body. Just as an initiate would proceed through the various chambers and ceremonies in the ancient temple, leading him or her to purity, wisdom, and holiness, so would one move one's consciousness and energy through the various chambers within one's body, a process of meditation, leading to purity, wisdom, and holiness.

Mysticism also teaches that the human body has seven spiritual centers or chakras within it, physically operating through the seven endocrine glands. Not surprisingly, ancient temples often have sevens reflected in elements of their design, as we will see in the first temple of ancient Egypt.

Here are a few of the temples in Egypt which reflect mystical truths. The main reason for studying these is to better understand one's own body as a temple.

ABYDOS, the head

In the myth of Osiris, his evil brother Set cuts Osiris's body into many parts; legend has it that the head of Osiris was buried at the Abydos temple, making it the highest and most sacred of temples. In a manner of speaking, it was the Mecca, the Jerusalem, the holy city of ancient Egypt.

In addition to having the traditional courtyard and hypostyle hall, this temple has seven sanctuaries instead of the usual single or occasional triune arrangement. These seven sanctuaries reflect the mystery of the seven spiritual centers of the body. Six of the seven sanctuaries have false doors on their back walls, but one has a real door that leads to the hidden, inner sanctuary of Osiris. Abydos's inner sanctuary has two parts: one enters the Holy Place first—to the right are three rooms, symbolic of the three levels of consciousness; to the left is the door that leads to the holy of holies, which also has three small adjacent rooms.

Each of the outer seven sanctuaries of Abydos represents one of the ancient gods, its particular role in the growth of the godlings, and the endocrine gland within the body.

SANCTUARY	GODLING	ROLE OR POWER	GLAND
1st	Seti	Satan, self-seeking one	Gonads
2nd	Ptah	Seat of the soul	Leydig cells
3rd	Harakhte	Warrior, challenger	Adrenals
4th	Amon-Ra	Hidden, unseen one	Thymus
5th	Osiris	Tester of the souls	Thyroid
6th	Isis	Conceiver of the messiah	Pineal
7th	Horus	Messiah, conqueror of Seti	Pituitary

The western side of the Abydos temple has shrines to the Osirian triad of Osiris, Isis, and Horus. These three represent, in order, the original consciousness, the bridging consciousness, and the redeemed consciousness.

EDFU, the mind

This temple is dedicated to the god Horus, the savior. His symbol is the falcon or hawk. He represents the higher mind. It has a huge courtyard, a magnificent hypostyle hall, and a sanctuary with the tabernacle and altar in place. In the courtyard, just before entering the hypostyle hall, is a huge granite statue of a falcon wearing two hats, one within the other. The outer hat is the red, angular hat of the ruler of Lower Egypt, symbolizing the lower self. The inner hat is the white, rounded hat of the ruler of Upper Egypt, symbolizing the higher self. The higher mind

can blend the human and divine consciousnesses of our being
in an eternal harmony.

This is a marvelous temple. Surrounding it is a high wall on
the inner side of which is carved the story of the struggle between good and evil, higher self and lower self, cooperation and
selfishness. With the help of all the gods of heaven, good overcomes evil, the higher self subdues the lower self, and cooperation rises above selfishness.

DENDERA, the heart

This temple is dedicated to the goddess Hathor, patron of
love, music, and dancing. Her glyph is the falcon or hawk of
Horus within a room, symbolizing that the place of the higher
mind (Horus) is in the heart (Hathor). In Egyptian mythology,
Hathor is the mate of Horus.

This temple has three sanctuaries, one each for Horus,
Hathor, and Iky. Its courtyard contains a statue of Bes, god of
music, childbirth, marriage, and domestic happiness, protector
of women in labor. It has twenty-four magnificent pylons in its
hypostyle hall. The temple also has the beautiful, circular zo-
diac of Egypt (a replica has replaced the original).

KOM OMBO, the twin forces

This unique temple, located on the edge of the ancient land
of Nubia, is divided into two: one half is dedicated to Horus the
Great, god of war (Haroeris), and the other to the crocodile god
Sobek, symbolizing the baser urges of the physical life. Here the
mind and the body struggle to coexist. Horus's half of the temple
runs along the left side, and Sobek's along the right. Each has its
own courtyard, hypostyle hall, and sanctuary with altar. If we
compare this arrangement with our bodies, we might note that
the right-brain hemisphere governs the left side of the body
(Horus's side of the temple), and the left hemisphere the right
side (Sobek's side).

This magnificent temple sits atop a hill on the bank of the
Nile, with a view in both directions: up to the higher country
and down to the lower. It is as if the builders are asking the

temple worshipers which direction do you choose to travel, or, like Isis, are you able to travel in both directions without losing your soul? Balancing the two great forces in one's being is what this temple is all about.

PHILAE, Isis's Flower on the Nile

Few goddesses are as revered as Isis. Hers is a compelling story that touches everyone. She gave so much of herself to help humanity subdue evil and reduce suffering. In Egyptian mythology, she is the conceiver of Horus, the savior from the reign of the evil Set, and she suffers much to bring Horus to his victorious destiny.

Hers is an island temple. Its outer courtyard is lined with magnificent pillars on both sides. The inner court is small, with a huge, hieroglyph-covered granite stone to the right of the steps leading into the hypostyle hall. Coptic Christians used this hypostyle hall during the Roman period. Their crosses are carved on the sandstone pylons and walls; an altar and a tabernacle still remain of their worship services. The walls show how they attempted to remove the visual voluptuousness of the ancient Egyptian goddess, scraping the sandstone away or covering it with mortar. Despite these attempts, the temple walls still reveal the beauty and expression of a more innocent time.

Just beyond the hall is the single sanctuary with an altar. One can stand at the head of the altar and look straight out through the hypostyle hall into the courtyard, sunlight penetrating the inner darkness of the small sanctuary.

This temple floor plan reflects the human body well, especially the female body. The outer courtyard, with its unique rows of pillars, are like two long legs. Its small, inner courtyard, with the birthing chamber just to the left of it, is like the abdomen with its womb. Then the hypostyle hall, with its riblike pylons, reflects the heart of the temple, where the worshipers spent much of their time (Egyptian and Christian). The dark, single sanctuary reflects the single-mindedness of its goddess, despite all the challenges placed before her. Her eye was truly single, seeking only the light of heavenly victory.

The ancient temples reflect the inner temple. Anyone who

truly grasps this truth and budgets a little time during the day to move his or her consciousness and energy through one's temple will find oneself purer, wiser, and holier (in the best sense of that word).

6

INITIATION

SELECTED TEXTS FROM THE
BOOK OF THE MASTER OF THE HIDDEN PLACES

The following text is taken from what is commonly referred to as *The Egyptian Book of the Dead*. However, a more exact translation of its title would be: *The Book of the Master of the Hidden Places*. I have selected excerpts that reveal mystical concepts, practices, and thoughts which lead the seeker through the transition from earth-consciousness to heaven-consciousness. My interpretation is explained in the footnotes, as well as some key concepts relating to the text. All of the text of this section of the ancient book corresponds to the passage through the halls and chambers within the Great Pyramid of Giza and to the "halls and chambers" within our bodies as we make the transition during meditation.

The **bold type** is the title or opening headline of the chapter or section in *The Egyptian Book of the Dead*; then follow excerpts of the translated text. Scattered within the body of this text you will see brackets with the words *[Person's Name]*. This is because the ceremony was personalized for each initiate. Often this ceremony was conducted with three priests, one leading the initiate and two just behind the initiate, speaking the words of the initiation aloud so that the initiate could hear them. The priests would speak the initiate's name at these key points in the ceremony. You can speak your name at these key moments in the ceremony.

Here begins the Entrance on Light, and of coming forth from and going into the Territory of the Holy Dead, in the beautiful Hidden Place.

Homage to thee, O Strong One[1] of the Hidden Place.

O you who make perfected souls to enter into the Temple of Reunion,[2] may you cause the perfected soul of the Reunited One, the seeker *[Person's Name]*,[3] to be victorious with you in the Temple of Reunion. May he/she hear as you hear; may he/she see as you see.

O you who open the way and lay open the paths to perfected souls in the Temple of Reunion, open you the way and lay open the paths to the soul of Reunited *[Person's Name]* ...

Homage to thee, O thou who art at the head of the Hidden Place,[4] thou Reunited One ... Grant that I may arrive in peace in the Hidden Place and that the lords of the Ascent may receive me.

The ... making (of) the Spirit Body to enter into the Upper Gate of the Ascent.[5]

Homage to thee, O thou that dwellest in the Holy Mountain[6] of the Hidden Place.

Entering on Light and living after death—

Hail, One, shining from the Moon! Hail, One shining from

---

[1]*Bull* is the literal symbol/word used here. Bull of Amentet is a common name for Osiris.

[2]The name *Osiris* is used here, but it means or symbolizes reunion of the separated parts.

[3]This is the personal name of the adept going through this initiation. Wherever you read this, replace it with your own name or the name of whoever is going through this initiation.

[4]In biospiritual anatomy, the head is the sanctuary, as explained in chapter 5.

[5]The Upper Gate is the pineal center, beginning at the root of the brain, extending through the crown chakra and over into the pituitary center.

[6]The Holy Mountain is the crown of the head and corresponds to the pineal gland.

the Moon! Grant that the Reunited *[Person's Name]* may come forth from among those multitudes which are outside; and let him/her be established as a dweller among the denizens[7] of heaven; and let the Hidden Places be opened unto him/her. And behold, Reunited One, Reunited *[Person's Name]*, shall Enter on Light.

... passing over the Celestial Road of the Upper Gate of the Tomb.
The Resurrected Infinite One, triumphant says: I open out a way over the Watery Abyss[8] which formeth a path between the two Combatants, Truth in Darkness and Truth in Light.[9]

... entering into and coming forth from the Hidden Place.
May a path be made for me whereby I may enter in peace into the beautiful Hidden Place ... and may a path be made for me whereby I may enter in and adore the Reunited One, the Lord of Life.
... praise to The Attuned One when he riseth upon the Horizon.

Here begin the praises and glorifyings of coming out from and of going into the glorious underworld which is in the beautiful Hidden Place.
I am Yesterday (the Timeless One); I know Today.

What then is this? It is the Hidden Place wherein were created the souls of the gods when the Father was leader in the Mountain of the Hidden Place.

I know the God who dwelleth therein. Who then is this? It is the Reunited One.

What then is this? It is the horizon of his Father, the Unmanifested One.

What then is this? It is the cutting off of the corruptible in the

[7]The literal Latin meaning *(de intus)* means "from within." Generally, it means a frequenter of a particular place, an inhabitant. Here it speaks of those who frequently enter into the heaven of their deeper consciousness.
[8]Genesis 1:2: " . . . and darkness was upon the face of the deep; and the Spirit of God was moving upon the waters." The ancient Egyptians sought a way over the "watery abyss" which separated flesh from spirit, earth from heaven, humankind from God. The "watery abyss" corresponds to the vast realms of the unconscious mind.
[9]The two combatants are Law and Love, Truth and Mercy, Spirit and Flesh. They are symbolized in the two great halls of the Pyramid, the hall of "Truth in Darkness" and the hall of "Truth in Light."

body of the Reunited One, the earthly *[Person's Name]* . . .

It is the purification of Reunited *[Person's Name]* on the day of his/her birth.

I pass over the way, I know the head [pineal] of the Pool [lyden] of the Well of Life.

What then is this? It is the gate, the door . . . and it is the northern door of the tomb [pineal center, crown chakra]. Now as concerning the Pool [lyden center, second chakra] of the Well of Life, it is Abtu; it is the way by which his father, the Unseen One, travelleth when he goes forth to the Realms of Initiation.

Now the southern gate [second chakra] of the Ascent is the gate of the Pillars of He who rises. It is the gate where the god who rises lifts the disc of heaven. The gate of the northern [pineal center, beginning at the base of the brain and continuing through the brain to the third-eye center] is the Gate of the Great God. The northern gate of the Ascent is the two leaves [i.e., hemispheres of the brain] of the door through which the Unmanifested god passeth when he goeth forth to the Eastern Horizon of Heaven [i.e., back of head, over the crown of the head and on toward the forehead and the third eye].

The Chapter of Entering on Light in the Underworld.

I am Yesterday, Today and Tomorrow, the Dweller in Eternity, (and I have) the power to be born a second time. (I am) the divine hidden Soul who . . . giveth meals unto the denizens of the Underworld, the Beautiful Hidden Place and heaven.

I am the Lord of seekers who are raised up; (the Lord) who cometh forth from out of the unconscious.

(Hail) Lord of the Shrine which standeth in the middle of the Earth. He is I, and I am He.

Make thou thy roads glad for me.

Send forth thy light upon me, O Soul unknown, for I am (one) of those who are about to enter in.

Come thou who (dwellest) above the divine Abyss of water.

The god who is the Conductor of Souls transporteth me to the Chamber of rebirth and (my) nurse is the divine double Lion-God himself, Yesterday and Tomorrow. I am made strong and I come forth like him that forceth a way through the gate . . . "I know the depths" is thy name.

Ancient Egyptian Mysticism

Illustrations

1. Gods, Goddesses, and Humans [front cover]

This colorful mural on the walls of Amen-her-Khopsef's tomb in the Valley of the Queens shows the interplay between gods and humans or, from a mystical perspective, the interplay between each soul's own human and divine parts. One may interpret these images as separate individuals (a Pharaoh, a goddess, etc.) or different aspects of one person. For example, the Pharaoh and goddess embracing may also represent the male and female aspects within each person. The young heir with his princely lock of hair, preceded by the mature Pharaoh offering incense to the blue-skinned god, mystically represents stages of enlightenment within each soul. The blue-skinned god represents the divine aspect that has been suspended during the predominance of physical life but will eventually awaken for eternity. The thoughts and actions of one's incarnate self are like incense that either enlivens or dulls the senses of our divine nature.

2. Mystical Images on Tomb Wall

These colorful walls of the tomb of the ancient artisan Sennedjem in the Valley of the Artisans are covered with beautiful mystical images. They each have two meanings, two messages. One is the physical and the other is the spiritual, mystical. In this book we examine more closely some of these fascinating and revealing images.

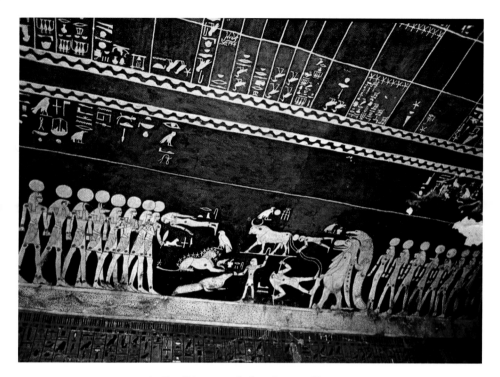

4. Godlings and the Constellations

On this ceiling in the tomb of Seti I, we see godlings with disks on their heads, indicating their god-conscious nature. These are the godlings who were first created in the image of the Creator. In the middle of them are some of the constellations of stars above the earth. These star clusters represent energy centers which have influence upon those in this dimension. They also represent specific strengths or talents that a godling needs to develop. To the right side, we see a hippo with a crocodile on its back. The hippo represents the large, submerged aspect of true life that awakens only when one raises up one's earthly crocodile nature–as one would one's kundalini energy or primal energy within, which runs up one's back along the path taken by this curious crocodile.

3. Godlings in the Heavens
(Opposite Page)

Prior to physical evolution through matter, there was spiritual involution into matter. On this ceiling in the tomb of Ramses VI in the Valley of the Kings, we see heavenly godlings in the many mansions of heaven or the spirit dimensions. In the legend of the fall of the angels, our divine selves, created in the image of the Creator, descended from heaven into earth, or matter, dying to heavenly things and dimensions and giving life to our physical things.

5. The Two Worlds—1

On the walls of Sennedjem's beautiful tomb in the Valley of the Artisans, we see this illustration of the two worlds. Sennedjem and his wife pay homage to the unseen world of the deeper consciousness and nonphysical life. This physical life, when understood properly, is preparation for the next life in the other world.

6. The Two Worlds—2

In the little tomb next to Sennedjem's is the tomb of Anherkhau (Inherka) with this beautiful illustration on its walls. Osiris sits on his throne, guarding the way between the outer world and the inner world. The all-seeing eye, in the watery dimension of the inner world, holds a container of incense cones that scent Osiris's flail, to calm his negative urges and uplift his spirit. The hawk, also in the watery dimensions, represents the higher mind, that which can fly above earthly desires and interests to see from a greater perspective.

7. Osiris with Symbols

A young Osiris, with his prince's lock of hair, holds some powerful symbols in his hands. The crook is the mystical symbol of the kundalini pathway. The kundalini is often represented by a raised serpent, a shepherd's staff, and, as we see here, a ruler's crook-ended staff. The flail symbolizes control over one's urges and senses. The tall, blue staff with the head of a jackal is the symbol of intuitive guidance, as described later in the caption for Anubis (#10). Below the jackal-head staff is the ankh, symbol for life. Below this is the symbol for stability, often called "the backbone of Osiris." Above Osiris's head are the moon and sun symbols, representing his consciousness. He has the light of the source of light (the sun) and can reflect it (the moon) even when in the dark underworld. On his chest is the sacred tabernacle that seals his heart against evil. On his forehead is the raised cobra, indicating the power of his raised kundalini energy. His blue skin indicates his spiritual nature. Red skin is the flesh with blood in it. Pale skin is the fair nature of the fairer sex, and green skin is the ghostly self that abides for a time in or near the underworld. It is a nonphysical but not yet fully spiritualized aspect of ourselves.

8. Pharaoh Inhales Ra's Powers

Here we see the human aspect of one's self inhaling the powers of the higher self: first, the white-centered ankh of life; second, the stabilizing nature of our higher self's backbone, needed to make the long journey of life; and finally, the intuitive guidance needed to find the forgotten way home.

9. Boat of Ra with Raised Serpent

In the tomb of Ramses I, we have this wonderful image of Ra in his boat, with a raised serpent that is blowing bubbles of new consciousness, a powerful way to convey the raised kundalini's influence on consciousness.

10. Anubis

One of the most fascinating and important gods in ancient Egypt is Anubis, symbolized by a jackal. Here is a beautifully carved, wooden statue from Tutankhamen's tomb, painted black and gilded with gold. Several of the important Egyptian gods have animal heads. This has nothing to do with animal worship. Each animal's primary skill or instinct represents the god's particular ability or role. In the case of Anubis, he is the guide through the underworld. He is a major part of all death and final judgment scenes. Why? If our souls have taken a long journey from home, from heaven, and we have lost our way back, our jackals have the ability, the power, to pick up the scent of the path we have taken and lead us back through the darkness to home again. This is why this god is so important. Within each of us is the intuitive sixth sense that will help us recall from where we have come and to where we must return. The darkness of death, sleep, or, for that matter, deep prayer or meditation, need not be difficult to traverse if we have the powerful help of Anubis—our own inner sense of the way through the darkness to the inner light on the other side, in the other, inner world.

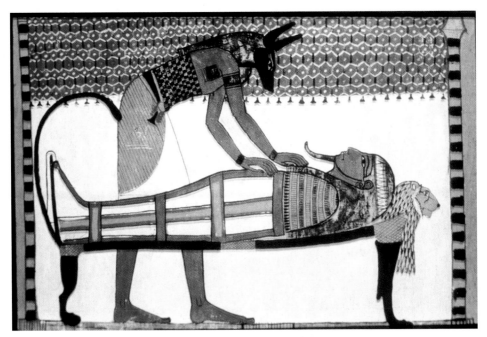

11. Anubis over Sennedjem

One of the fine images on the walls of Sennedjem's tomb is the great god Anubis bending over Sennedjem's mummy, getting ready to lead Sennedjem through the underworld to the heavens.

12. Hermes

On this pillar in the tomb of Ramses IV, we find this excellent painted carving of one of the greatest gods in Egypt, Hermes. Hermes is the Greek name for this god; Thoth is the Egyptian. Here we see him represented with the head of an ibis. The ibis is a bird who lives along the shore, between the two worlds of the deep water and the land, symbolizing Hermes's ability to live between two worlds, the deep unconscious inner world and the outer conscious one. Upon his head are the symbols of sun and moon, meaning he knows the source of light and life and can reflect it when out of direct contact with it. Animal heads always symbolize the special abilities of the god.

13. Hermes with Two Staffs

The great Hermes holds two staffs in his hand. One is the lotus staff of enlightenment, and the other is the papyrus staff of wisdom. Around the staffs, the cobra rises as the kundalini within the body, drawn by the fragrance of these two blossoms. On the heads of the cobras are the hats of their status. The angular hat symbolizes the lower self, ruler of Lower Egypt and the earthly portion of our being. The rounded hat symbolizes the higher self, ruler of Upper Egypt, and the heavenly portion of our being. In his other hand, Hermes places the ankh of eternal life to the nose of Pharaoh, who inhales the power that has resulted from this attunement.

14. Winged Serpent

Serpents are a powerful symbol for the life force of a person. In India, this is called the kundalini energy. In China, it is called chi. The West calls it *elan vital* or simply the life force. The position or features of the serpent indicate the nature of the life force. In this illustration, we have a winged serpent, as is also found in Mayan art. The winged serpent symbolizes the life force raised by the mind's ability to fly above this world into thoughts and ideals above the mundane, earthly needs and concerns. Here we see the winged serpent drawn on a coffin in the Cairo Museum. Death is the ultimate release from earthly concerns. The disk symbolizes god-consciousness, indicating how the life force lives on beyond death if mindfulness is awakened to the spiritual consciousness. Then, the life force is strong, even beyond death.

15. Raised Serpent

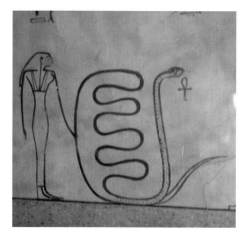

In Genesis, the serpent falls from grace and out of the Tree of Life, to crawl on its belly through the earth realm. To raise up the serpent again is one of the greatest achievements because the serpent symbolizes the life force within us. This life force fell from grace and power as our souls descended from heaven to enter the earth realms. While here, we must raise that energy in order to fully realize our true nature. Jesus indicates this secret teaching in His comments to Nicodemus: "As Moses raised the serpent in the desert so must I be raised up to eternal life." (John 3:14) Moses raised the serpent when he first met God in the burning bush. God instructed him to raise the serpent off the desert floor and, as he did, the serpent became a powerful staff. Here on the wall in the tomb of a Pharaoh, we find this powerful teaching. The looping tail symbolizes the spiritual centers within our bodies that are profoundly affected by raising the life force to higher levels than normally needed to exist physically. In Eastern teachings, raising the kundalini through the chakras within the body results in enlightenment. Ancient Egypt taught the same mystery to its initiates. This illustration is on the wall of the tomb of Tutmose III.

16. Sennedjem's Mystical Eyes

On this beautiful wall in Sennedjem's tomb (sometimes spelled *Senngem*) is this important mystical teaching. Between the eye of Ra and the eye of Horus lies the secret place of the white disk of divine light. Around the white light is the circular symbol for eternity, tied to the linear rod of temporality. This reflects a sacred union between the infinite and finite. Out of this union comes the wavy lines, symbolizing the water of life pouring into the cup of life. All these mystical symbols recall to the initiate's mind the true point on the forehead of each seeker's body where the Creator meets the created, giving life in the midst of death, eternity in the midst of temporality, the infinite in the midst of the finite.

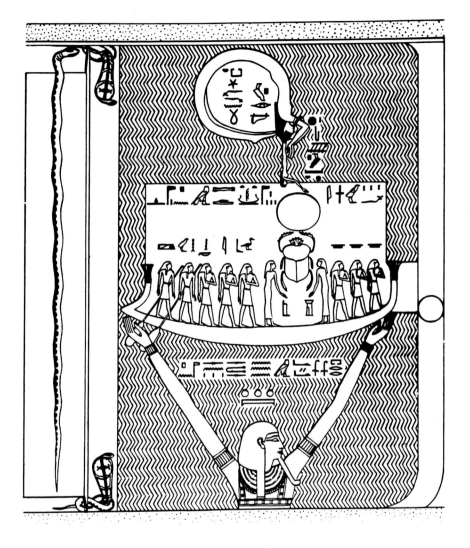

17. Creation

The circle or disk is the symbol of God. Here we have the circle of God's consciousness formed by the spirit and power of women. She conceives a child in her image out of her crown chakra, giving it life to know and love God and all of creation. The child honors the solar disk of God. Below this scene is another world that is upside down from the godly realm and is traveling through time and space on a boat, but the boat sails toward a solar disk, too. On the boat, a scarab, symbol of earthliness and the lowest levels of life, honors the solar disk of God, too. Below the scarab are Isis and Nephthys, with the symbols for the throne of God and the magic bowl of God. The goddess of creation holds up the boat of life, keeping it from the great abyss of eternal darkness, lost forever from god-consciousness. All of this occurs in the watery dimensions of inner consciousness. To the left of the scene, we see the great raised serpent, symbolizing the power and life of the raised kundalini force within each entity.

18. Entering and Exiting the Earth—1

In Ramses VI's tomb, we have this complex wall illustration. Look to the center area and you will see two lions. Above them, you will see two boats, one coming down into the earth and the other rising out of the earth.

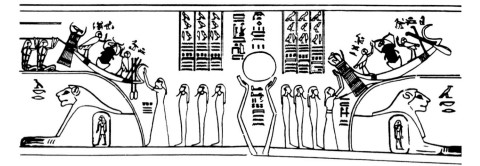

19. Entering and Exiting the Earth—2

Here is a line drawing of the previous illustration from the wall of Ramses VI's tomb.

20. Chromosome Structure—1

Out of this body on the walls of Ramses IV's tomb, we see a double helix weaving its way around the wall. At each crossing of the helix, glyphs indicate which part of the body this portion of the chromosome controls.

21. Chromosome Structure—2

This line illustration allows us to see the double-helix pattern coming out of a body.

22. Androgyny of the Soul

In this wall picture, we see the soul with breast and phallus to convey the androgyny of the soul. The blue skin confirms that this is not an incarnate body with flesh and blood, but a spiritual body beyond the earthly being. The little child reveals the secret teaching that this soul portion of our being is the heir, the prince who will some day inherit the life from the physical self and live with God in the kingdom of heaven forever. The two circles represent two levels of consciousness, one seen and one unseen, deep within or behind the evident.

23. The Open Mystical Pyramid

On a wall in the tomb of Tal Wasre, we find this amazing illustration of an open pyramid. At the top we have the arms of God giving the consciousness of God in the form of the red Ra disk. Then we have the sacred scarab rolling his dross into a new red disk, representing a new consciousness that reflects the original one. All of this is occurring above an altar that is tended by human-bodied beings and bird-bodied beings, representing the two parts of our being, human and soul. The whole scene is above the head of the ram god, Khnum, representing Aries and the beginning of time.

24. Open Mystical Pyramid —right side

Here's a closer look at the right side of the open pyramid. Notice how they have separated the pyramid into three different sections. The top section is black, representing the infinite realms of space and the higher dimensions. The middle section is blue with wavy lines, representing the watery world of the unseen, the underworld. The lowest section is the white world of physical life. In this section, we see the black, round primeval mound of the first land, with a gold chalice carved on it.

25. Soul in Mother's Arms

In this illustration, we have a woman holding a ba, a bird-bodied human representing the soul. This soul has just come from heaven to begin its incarnation in the physical world.

26. The Story of the Souls

Descending into a tomb, we see this strange row of human-headed birds with their arms giving homage to the forces or gods on the other side of death. The human-headed bird is called the "ba." It represents one's soul, that part of one that can "fly" above this life yet retain one's individual persona. Death is only a transition for one's soul, a journey through the shadow of death into realms of nonphysical life.

27. Horus Weighing the Heart

One of the greatest scenes in ancient Egypt is the judgment scene. It is found in many places and on many papyri. Here we see one small section of the whole story, the weighing of the heart by the higher mind, represented by Horus. The heart is in the jar, and it is being weighed against a feather—not just any feather, but the feather of truth and justice, the icon of the goddess Maat, the female counterpart to Hermes.

28. Weighing the Heart—left side

In the first stage of death, the heart of the deceased is placed into a jar and weighed against the feather of truth. If the heart is light, then the soul passes on to the heavens. If the heart is heavy, then the beast at the foot of the scale eats it, and the soul is heavy with unfinished business or desires of this world. It struggles through many challenges in the underworld, to rise again like the sun on a new dawn, a new life, to resolve its weighty concerns and desires. In this illustration, we see that Ani's heart is lighter than the feather, and Horus points the way beyond the scale to Osiris's throne. See the next illustration.

29. Weighing the Heart—right side

His heart having been found light, Ani is presented before the god of the underworld, Osiris. Behind Osiris stand Isis and her sister, Nephthys. This trinity represents purity, rebirth, and magic. On the lotus blossom in front of Osiris, we see the "four children of Horus" who represent the four lower urges of physical life, the four lower chakras, and the four beasts of Ezekiel, Daniel, and The Revelation. These urges are wrapped like mummies, indicating their subdued influence at this spiritual time. In the depiction of this same scene on the walls in the temple at Abydos is another stage of death beyond the throne of Osiris. On those walls, we see the deceased move through and behind Osiris's little shrine into the heavens, where the gods meet the deceased and guide him or her to new levels of life.

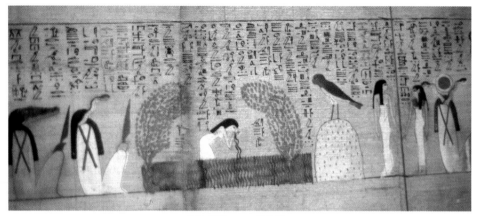

30. Water of Life

On this papyrus, we see a deceased woman in heaven drinking the Water of Life, while the Trees of Life bend toward her, offering their fruit. Again, we see the raised serpent as a symbol of the elevated kundalini life force. We see the wrapped crocodile symbolizing the subdued lower urges. And we see everything in white, conveying the purity of the moment. This woman's soul perches on the primordial stone, watching over her spiritual nourishment.

32. Papyrus with Raised Serpent

The raised serpent is an ancient symbol of the raised kundalini and its power. On this papyrus, we see Horus, the resurrected mind, with his kundalini life force raised up his spine, over his head, and fully present before his forehead and eyes. The solar disk above his head shows that his mind is filled with the consciousness of God. Before him stand the goddesses Hathor (love and beauty) and Maat (truth and justice). In his hands are an ankh (life) and the wisser staff (strength, power, and guidance). On the bow of his boat is the all-seeing eye of Ra, guiding his way across the waters of the firmament to the heavens.

31. Papyrus with Soul and Ghost

On this papyrus, we see the ghost of an entity pass through God's other door into the nonphysical realm of the soul, depicted by the human-headed bird with its wings spread for flight. The yang-ish solar disk of the outer, projected physical life is now the yin-ish black disk of the underworld and inner, nonphysical life.

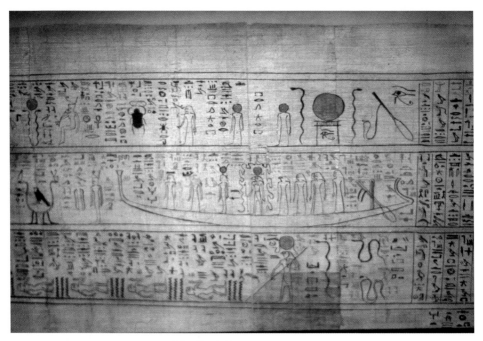

33. God-Consciousness

On this image-rich papyrus, we see human bodies with solar disks for heads, the ultimate image of God-consciousness. Many of the symbols we have studied in this book are depicted on this fascinating papyrus: all-seeing eye, raised serpents, scarabs, hawks, crowns of higher self and lower self, and so on.

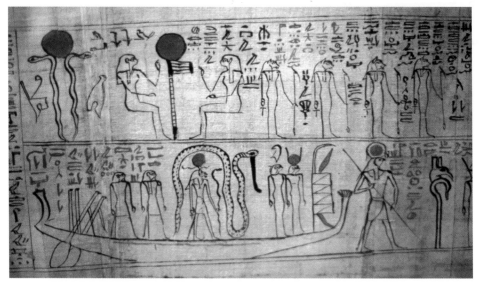

34. Mystical Papyrus

Here are more wonderfully symbolic images of mystical forces that influence life, death, and transformation. In the lower right-hand corner, we have the head of Satan, Set, upon a crook, indicating the Egyptians' belief in the redemption of even this evil god.

35. Horus Temple Courtyard

One of the three key parts of an Egyptian temple is the open courtyard, representing the abdominal cavity in the body temple of each human being. Horus represents the higher mind in the form of a falcon that can fly higher above the earth and see from a different perspective in great detail. See chapter 5.

36. Hathor Osiris Chapel

Outside the main temple of Hathor, goddess of love and beauty, we find magnificent mini-temples devoted to birth, death, and resurrection. On the walls of these chapels are depictions of how the gods in heaven help guide souls from this world to the next. In the birthing chapel, the images show how the gods help with conception, soul selection, and physical body formation. See chapter 5.

37. Kom Ombo Hypostyle Hall

One of the three key parts of an Egyptian temple is the pillared hall, representing the pulmonary cavity with its ribs in the body temple of each human being. This is the strange temple of duality on the border of Nubia in Kom Ombo. It is dedicated to the struggle between the higher mind (Horus) and the lower self (Sobek). See chapter 5.

38. Isis Temple from the Water

This is the only island temple in Egypt. Om Seti called it the "Pearl of the Nile." Dedicated to the goddess Isis, it is one of the most beautiful temples in Egypt. It is located in Aswan on Philae Island. Isis's consciousness, depicted on her head, is the throne of God. She is one of the most important goddesses of ancient Egypt. She immaculately conceives the savior Horus, who ultimately overthrows the selfish ruler Set. See chapter 5.

39. Isis Temple Courtyard See chapter 5.

40. Sphinx with Dream Stela

Look closely at this stela and you will see a large, roomlike structure beneath the Sphinxes. Could this be a secret message from the dreaming Pharaoh that there is a hidden Hall of Records beneath the great Sphinx? (Photo by Rufus Mosely.)

41. Sphinx Statue, Normal

Here is a normal, human-headed sphinx. Compare this with the next photo of a very different sphinx.

42. Sphinx Statue, Tunis

Is this a remnant of Atlantis? Notice how much more the animal influence is present in this image. Notice also the very different shape to the face, compared with the previous sphinx photo. This sphinx was found in Tunis.

43. Sphinx and the Second Pyramid (Opposite Page)

Notice the causeway leading from the Sphinx to the second pyramid. Initiates would begin their transformation in the Valley Temple next to the Sphinx, then progress up the causeway to the "funerary" temple on the east side of the pyramid for further training, and then on into the pyramid's main entrance on the north side. Once inside the pyramid, they would go through the various ceremonies in the inner chambers, ultimately going into the open sarcophagus for the final initiation that would lead to victory over death and to eternal life.

44. Misty Pyramids

In the 1930s, Edgar Cayce said that Giza was laid out according to the stars above it, but it wasn't until the early '90s that this was confirmed with the research and publication of *The Orion Mystery* by Adrian Gilbert and Robert Bauval. The Giza plateau is one of the rare, magical places on this planet.

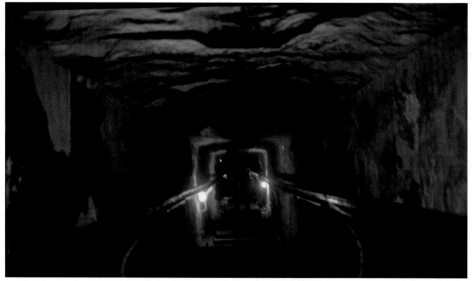

45. Hall of Truth in Darkness

This is the low, narrow passageway that leads up toward the Queen's and King's Chambers in the Great Pyramid. According to *The Egyptian Book of the Dead*, its name is actually the "Hall of Truth in Darkness."

46. Grand Gallery and Queen's Chamber

As one exits the Hall of Truth in Darkness, this is what lies ahead. Looking straight ahead, you see the low, narrow passageway to the Queen's Chamber, which *The Egyptian Book of the Dead* calls "The Chamber of the Second Birth." As you look upward, you see the steps leading to the King's Chamber.

47. Hall of Truth in Light

This is the large, grand gallery of the Great Pyramid. *The Egyptian Book of the Dead* calls this passageway the "Hall of Truth in Light." This is a view looking back down the hall from the "Great Step."

48. Sarcophagus with Light Rays

After our group meditated in the King's Chamber, we took some photos of the sarcophagus. Whether these patterns are simply camera quirks or energy patterns, I cannot say. But something was affecting the film in my camera, and it only did it while I was in the King's Chamber.

49. Ani Rises from His Coffin

There was no death in ancient Egypt, simply a transition to other realms of life. See chapter 4.

50. Ani's Ba (Soul) Leaves His Body   See chapter 4.

51. Anubis Guides the Dead to the Other Side   See chapter 4.

52. Ani Encourages His Soul to Enter the Gate and Rise   See chapter 4.

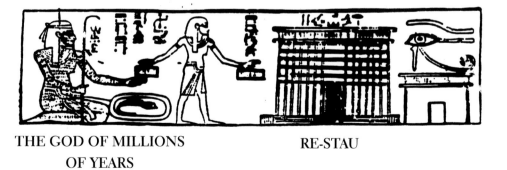

THE GOD OF MILLIONS
OF YEARS

RE-STAU

53. The Lower and Upper Gates   See chapter 4.

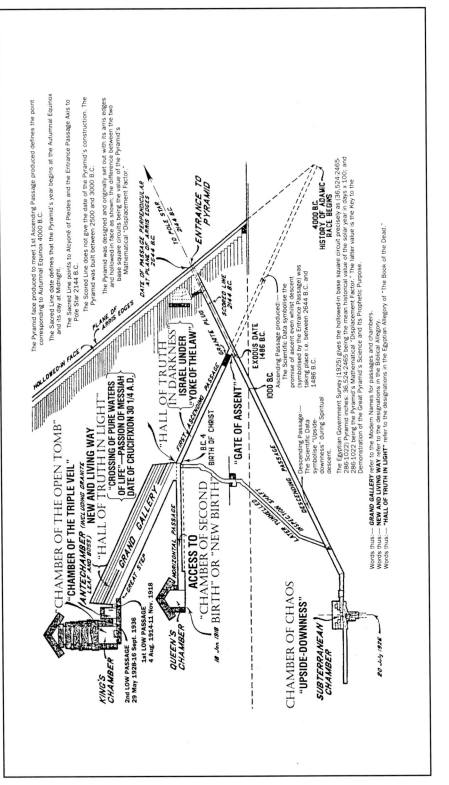

The Pyramid face produced to meet 1st Ascending Passage produced defines the point corresponding to Autumnal Equinox 4000 B.C.

The Sacred Line date defines that the Pyramid's year begins at the Autumnal Equinox and its day at Midnight.

The Sacred Line points to Alcyoné of Pleides and the Entrance Passage Axis to Pole Star 2144 B.C.

The Scored Line does not give the date of the Pyramid's construction. The Pyramid was built between 2500 and 3000 B.C.

The Pyramid was designed and originally set out with its arris edges and hollowed-in face as shown; the difference between the two base square circuits being the value of the Pyramid's Mathematical "Displacement Factor."

PLANE OF ARRIS EDGES

HOLLOWED-IN FACE

DATE OF PASSAGE PERPENDICULAR AT PLANE OF ARRIS EDGES 2644 BC

TO POLE STAR 2144 BC

ENTRANCE TO PYRAMID

SCORED LINE 2144 BC

GRANITE PLUG

"HALL OF TRUTH IN DARKNESS" ISRAEL UNDER "YOKE OF THE LAW"

FIRST ASCENDING PASSAGE

"CHAMBER OF THE OPEN TOMB"

"CHAMBER OF THE TRIPLE VEIL"

ANTECHAMBER (INCLUDING GRANITE LEAF AND BOSS) NEW AND LIVING WAY "HALL OF TRUTH IN LIGHT"

"CROSSING OF PURE WATERS OF LIFE" — PASSION OF MESSIAH DATE OF CRUCIFIXION 30 1/4 A.D.

GRAND GALLERY

GREAT STEP

HORIZONTAL PASSAGE

ACCESS TO "CHAMBER OF SECOND BIRTH" OR "NEW BIRTH"

B.C.4 BIRTH OF CHRIST

"GATE OF ASSENT"

EXODUS DATE 1486 BC

1000 BC

Ascending Passage produced:—
The Scientific Data symbolise the promise of ascent even whilst descent (symbolised by the Entrance Passage) was taking place i.e. between 2644 B.C. and 1486 B.C.

4000 B.C. HISTORY OF ADAMIC RACE BEGINS

The Egyptian Government Survey (1925) gives the hollowed-in base square circuit precisely as (36,524.2465-286.1022) Pyramid inches: 36,524.2465 being the mean historical value of the solar year in days x 100; and 286.1022 being the Pyramid's Mathematical "Displacement Factor." The latter value is the Key to the Demonstration of the Great Pyramid's Science and its Prophetic Purpose.

KING'S CHAMBER

2nd LOW PASSAGE 29 May 1928-16 Sept. 1936

1st LOW PASSAGE 4 Aug. 1914-11 Nov. 1918

QUEEN'S CHAMBER

18 Jan 1918

CHAMBER OF CHAOS "UPSIDE-DOWNNESS"

SUBTERRANEAN CHAMBER

20 July 1926

DESCENDING PASSAGE

INSPECTION SHAFT

LATER TUNNELLED

Descending Passage:—
The Scientific Data symbolise "Upside-downness" during Spiritual descent.

Words thus:— **GRAND GALLERY** refer to the Modern Names for passages and chambers.
Words thus:— **NEW AND LIVING WAY** refer to the designations in the Biblical Allegory.
Words thus:— **HALL OF TRUTH IN LIGHT** refer to the designations in the Egyptian Allegory of "The Book of the Dead."

54. David Davidson's Interpretative Illustration of the Great Pyramid   See chapter 8.

I am he who Entereth on Light.

The doors of heaven are opened for me, the doors of earth are opened for me.

Hail, thou soul who risest in heaven.

Strengthen thou me according as thou hast strengthened thyself, and show thyself upon earth, O thou that returnest and withdrawest thyself.

Messiah, Redeemer, son of the Mother of all, avenger of the Father! Strengthen thou me, according as thou hast strengthened thyself, and show thyself upon earth, O thou that returnest and withdrawest thyself.

The Chapter of causing the soul to be united to its body in the Underworld.

The Reunited *[Person's Name]*, triumphant, says: Hail, thou god "the bringer"! Hail, thou god "the runner," who dwellest in thy hall! Great God! Grant thou that my soul may come unto me from wheresoever it may be.

Hail, ye gods . . . who make souls to enter into (their) spiritual bodies . . . grant ye that the soul of Reunited *[Person's Name]*, triumphant, may come forth before the gods . . . and that it may have peace in the Hidden Place. May it look upon its body and neither perish nor suffer corruption for ever.

The paths which are above me lead to the gateway.

Open unto me! Who then art thou? Whither goest thou? What is thy name?

The Chapter of entering into the Hall of Double Truth.

And they say unto me, who art thou then? and they say unto me, what is thy name?

Come, then, they say, and enter in through the door of this Hall of Double Truth.

We will not let thee enter in through us, say the bolts of this door, unless thou tellest (us) our names.[10] Tongue (of the Bal-

---

[10]Naming the name is a very ancient practice. It requires that the initiate intuit from within him- or herself the truth. Recall when Jesus asked Peter who he thought Jesus was, and Peter, answering correctly, was rewarded with the compliment: "Blessed are you, Simon, for flesh and blood did not tell you this, but the spirit revealed it to you." (Matt. 16:17)

ance) of the place of right and truth is your name.

The heavens are opened, the earth is opened, the West is opened, the East is opened, the southern half of heaven is opened, the northern half of heaven is opened.

The Chapter of forcing an entrance into heaven.

The Attuned One liveth, the Earth Bound One dieth. Sound is he who is the chest, Reunion triumphant. This Book is the Greatest of Mysteries. Do not let the eye of anyone look upon it—that is abomination. *The Book of the Master of the Hidden Places* is its name.

May those who build up grant that the Reunited *[Person's Name]* shall arrive happily in the Hall of Double Truth.

May He Who Makes Reunion to be Secret grant that the Reunited *[Person's Name]* may be a lord of strides in the habitation of the Ascent.

And there shall be made an offering by the Reunited *[Person's Name]* when he entered through the hidden pylons.

May the company of the gods who rule over the Hidden Place grant that Reunited *[Person's Name]* shall go in through the secret door of the House of Reunion.

And there shall be made . . . an offering . . . by Reunited *[Person's Name]* when he shall walk up the Great Staircase.

The Lady of the Hidden Place, mighty dweller in the funeral mountain, lady of the Holy Place receive the Reunited *[Person's Name]*.[11]

---

[11]This lady corresponds with the woman in St. John's Revelation in chapter 12, where John describes seeing a divine lady wrapped in the sun, standing on the moon, with twelve stars over her head. She is pregnant and gives birth to the deliverer in the midst of the great red dragon.

7

Mystical Anatomy
The Secret Parts of Our Being

The physical body in ancient Egypt was much the same as we have today. Mystically speaking, most of the ancient Egyptians were in Adamic bodies (i.e., bodies descended from Adam). According to Edgar Cayce's reading of the akashic records, the body created by Yahweh Elohim in the second chapter of Genesis was the prototype for the Western human race. The Cayce reading of the records states that the children of God descended from spirit into matter in five distinct groups, one of these groups was called "Adam." Adam is both a specific individual and a large soul-group. Cayce says that the races entered the Earth plane in five specific areas. The Gobi desert region (it was fertile then, not desert) was the entry point of the yellow race. The Andean mountain range, down into the Pacific coast areas of what is today South America and vast areas of the Pacific, was the legendary land of Lemuria or "The Motherland Mu," entry point for the brown race. In Atlantis, the red race entered the plane on a large continent in the Atlantic, stretching from the modern eastern shore of the U.S. and Bahamas to the Azores. In the Sudan of Africa, along the great Congo River (very fertile in ancient times, no deserts) was the entry point for the black race, a land called Nubia. In the Carpathian and Caucasian Mountains down upon the plain where the Tigris and Euphrates Rivers flow, the white race entered.

This body type that we possess today can be found, in virtually identical form, in remains dating as far back as 400,000 years ago. The structure of all humanoid remains older than 400,000 years are different from ours today. Therefore, one can assume that something changed about 400,000 years ago, and that change is still with us. Fascinatingly, Cayce and others predict that we are on the verge of another major change in the physical body, a new body type, what Cayce calls the fifth root race.

In addition to the body, most of us would agree that we have minds, emotions, souls, and spirits or ghosts. The ancient Egyptians identified nine parts of a person (the number varied at times, but the following nine are standard):

1. the physical body   khat or kha
2. the heart   ab
3. the shadow   khaibit or shut
4. the name   ren
5. the soul   ba
6. the mind   khu or akh
7. the spirit-body   sahu
8. the spirit   ka
9. the power   sekhem

The physical body, *kha,* is the fleshy part of our body and is represented in hieroglyphics by a fish and a nose, as if to say that this is the smelly part of our being. But there is much more to this glyph than smell. The fish is not found on any of the feast-table scenes in ancient Egypt because it is believed to be the creature that ate Osiris's phallus, the one part of his body that was never recovered by Isis. Thus, the fish is not welcomed at the offering table or banquet table. It is as though the physical body is the part encased in the vitality of the soul (symbolized by the phallus). Also, the nose is representative of the breath of life required to bring the physical body to life, as written in the second chapter of Genesis.

The heart, *ab*, is the essential nature of the person: cold-hearted, warm-hearted, hard-hearted, soft-hearted, broken-hearted, big-hearted, and so on. As Jesus said, it's not what goes into a person that defiles him or her, it's what comes out, because that comes from the heart. In the Bible, the Lord frequently said that He wanted to give humans "a new heart" or "circumcise their hearts." This makes sense when we consider that a "change of heart" is key to restoration of our divinity. The heart is the part of a person that is weighed in the balance at ancient Egyptian judgment scenes. In the scene, the heart is placed in a jar, put on a scale, and weighed against a feather, symbolic of the delicate nature of truth. If the heart is true, weighing in lightly from lack of guilt or unresolved concerns, then the person may continue on to the heavens.

The shadow, *shut*, pronounced "shoot," is that part of us that is revealed when we turn away from the Sun. It is an unseen portion of our being that is latent, and manifests itself when we are at our most vulnerable, such as in the transition from consciousness to unconsciousness; falling to sleep or dying would be two examples. It is our ghost. You'll see these images in ancient tomb scenes and in the illustrations of the hours of the night.

The name, *ren*, is our most individualizing identifier. According to the teachings, each soul has a unique name distinguishable from all the other millions of souls. Our name, that is our *soul* name, is who we are specifically from all the rest of God's creation. It is our unique identifier. It is not the name that we have on earth, but is the name by which the Universal God knows us. In the Scriptures it is said, "I call them by name." (Isaiah 40:26) And we see in The Revelation that St. John receives his holy name during his deep mystical experience—he sees it written on a white stone. Notice how the glyph for *name* is a mouth speaking over the water, perhaps indicating that this is the name we had above the firmament (as in Genesis 1:7, "a firmament divided the waters below from the waters above").

The soul, *ba*, is the individual part of us that survives death
and was originally given life by the Creator (see chapter 1 of
Genesis). The body was not created until later, as told in chapter
2. In ancient Egypt, the ba is most often drawn as a bird with a
human head wearing a priestlike skullcap. This indicates that
the soul is very much like our personality (the human head) but
is able to rise higher above the personality's perspective on life
(the bird). The skullcap indicates that it has a different mental
focus than the personality.

Cayce sees the soul as the inner developing part of our being.
He says that it is indeed like the personality but larger and im-
mortal, containing the memories and urges of the whole being,
not simply of the earthly self. The soul, according to Cayce, is
growing, becoming, according to what the personality feeds it.
It is the sum total of all we have done with our life. At death, the
soul takes over from the personality and is either strengthened
by the personality's life accomplishments or malnourished by
them. If the life was good, then it can rise to the higher heavens.
If not, then it may sink to the lower levels of the underworld.

The mind, the *khu*, is the savior of lost souls. With its ability
to live between the two worlds of heaven and earth, it forms the
bridge between our strictly physical selves and our heavenly
selves. The more the mind is nourished and developed and allowed to awaken, the more clearly we become aware of the
higher ideals and realms. These higher realms are not physical;
they are *dimensions of consciousness*. Therefore, consciousness
must be expanded. Mind is the savior. Mind is the builder. Mind
is the bridge from this island of consciousness to the universal,
infinite consciousness.

Unlike the physical body, the *sahu* or spirit body is energy,
not matter. Let's consider that all life is *energy* and *matter*—the
E and *m* of Einstein's great formula $E=mc^2$. Matter is simply the
physical manifestation of unseen energy. You can see how there
is no death: the dissipation of matter, such as the dying of a
physical body, is simply the transformation of its matter-condi-
tion to its energy-condition. The enlivening of matter with what
we call "life" is simply the imbuing of matter with the essential
energy of a godly being. When we go into deep meditation, we
transfer the focus from the matter of life to the energy, which is

the essence of matter. Flesh and spirit can easily be equated with matter and energy. The sahu is the energy body, the spirit body. It gives life to the physical body. If the sahu leaves or diminishes its presence in the physical body, then we see death or illness. The spirit is the life.

The spirit being, *ka*, is our highest state of beingness. It is our spirit-self, our angel-self. It is the twin or double of the individual. In ancient Egypt and in most cultures with a mystical tradition, there exists a legend of two brothers. One kills the other out of a self-seeking desire. However, in time, the lost one is restored and united with his contrite and humbled brother in the home of their birth. These are two beings within us. One is self-centered, seeking self-gratification and self-aggrandizement, the other is seeking oneness with the Whole, the Creator, and the creation.

The ka portion of our being is so attuned to the Universal Spirit that it is not nearly as personalized as our physical personage. It is more a part of God, a god within the God, remaining in the Oneness.

The power, *sekhem*, is the power to animate oneself when in the heavens. Without it we are unconscious or semiconscious, and therefore of little or no "lifeness" whenever we are not incarnate. This is the outer darkness into which the spirits asked Jesus not to send them. This is true death—not the death of the body, but the death of the nonembodied consciousness. Without the power to light this consciousness, our spirit-being (ka) is in darkness. That's when we are lost souls (ba) and the death of our bodies (khat) sends us, unconscious, to the dark underworld until we incarnate again. As long as we continue to lack the *sekhem*, the special power, to light our spirit consciousness, our physical death is a passage into the underworld, not the heavens. As Jesus put it in Matthew 6:23, "If the light that is in you is darkness, how great is that darkness!"

8

THE GREAT PYRAMID
A MASTERPIECE OF MATHEMATICS AND MYSTICISM

The pyramids at Giza are a testament to the ingenuity, vision, and wisdom of their builders. The Great Pyramid, so called because it is the tallest and the most complex of the three at Giza, has challenged all who have attempted to replicate it. To all who have gazed upon it, from engineers to mystics, the presence of ancient wisdom is obvious, but speculation as to what is being conveyed has filled volumes. Let us begin with the simple facts.

The Great Pyramid is situated ten miles to the southwest of Cairo, the capital of Egypt. It stands on the northern edge of the Giza Plateau, 198 feet above sea level, in the eastern extremity of the Sahara Desert. It is very close to the center of the land mass of the entire earth, which means that if one were to find which line of longitude and which line of latitude passes over more of the earth's surface than any other, they would cross at Giza! The Pyramid also happens to be at the apex of the Nile

delta. If one extends the diagonals of the Great Pyramid north-
ward, they would enclose the entire fan-shaped country of
Lower Egypt.

The Great Pyramid stands 454 feet high in its present state. Its
original height has been calculated to have been 485 feet, the
equivalent of a forty-eight-story skyscraper. The lengths of the
sides at its base average 755.75 feet, about one-seventh of a mile.
The base of the Pyramid sits on over thirteen acres of bedrock.

The Pyramid rests on a platform of carefully cut stones 21.6
inches thick that extend out beyond the base an average of 15.5
inches. This platform is perfectly square and level to within
eight-tenths of an inch, despite earthquakes and thousands of
years of weather.

The core of the Pyramid that we now see is of a yellow limestone quarried from across the Nile River just a few miles away.
It is estimated that there are over 2,300,000 of these blocks, the
average weight being two-and-one-half tons. Some weigh as
much as seventy tons, the equivalent of a railroad locomotive. If
the Pyramid were built in twenty years, as some ancient sources
have suggested, it would mean that 315 stones would need to
be placed each day. Working twelve hours a day, that would be
twenty-six stones each hour for the entire twenty years. If Edgar
Cayce were correct in saying that it took one hundred years to
build, that is still over five stones per hour for one hundred
years. It is a construction marvel.

The surface of the Great Pyramid, about 5.25 acres per side,
was originally covered by smooth white limestone. These casing stones, the edges of which are straight to within 1/100 of an
inch over a distance of 75 inches, are also fitted to each other
with uncanny precision. The joints between the stones average
only 1/50 of an inch in width and yet there is an extraordinarily
thin film of white cement between them that bonds the blocks
together. The average weight of these casing stones is sixteen
tons, yet the precision with which they were laid has been compared to the work of an optician on the scale of acres. Some authors have speculated that these highly polished limestone
sides of the Great Pyramid made it visible from the moon when
the sun's rays reflected from its surface. These stones were removed in the fourteenth century to build palaces and mosques

in Cairo. A few of the original casing stones remain on the north side of the Great Pyramid and on the top of the second pyramid.

The orientation of the Pyramid is no less marvelous than its construction. It is aligned with true north to within three minutes of a degree. The modern-day's best efforts at the Paris Observatory only came to within six minutes of a degree. Again, the Pyramid's accuracy has endured centuries of settling and earthquakes.

The inside of the Great Pyramid is no less fascinating than its outer magnificence. It is the only pyramid in Egypt with such highly elevated passages and rooms within the structure. It is also the only pyramid to have air vents. And, it is the only one to have a Grand Gallery. The fact that the three pyramids at Giza lack almost completely in ornamentation and that these three alone excel in size and construction techniques only adds to the mystery of their origin and purpose. To date, no original burials have been found in any pyramid in Egypt. In fact, in some pyramids original *sealed* coffins have been found but, when opened, were completely empty!

The entrance now used to enter the Great Pyramid is not the one placed there by the builders, but is a passage forced by Al Mamun, caliph of Cairo in the ninth century. The true entrance is above it on the same north face. Once through the original entrance, one enters into a descending passage that is only three feet eleven inches high and three feet six inches wide. This is set at an angle of twenty-six degrees and from the entrance descends 345 feet into the bedrock, ending in a strange chamber with a pit or well in it.

Shortly after entering the descending passage, one comes to an ascending passage that heads upward at exactly twenty-six degrees. The original granite plug that barred further entry was so hard that the chisels of Al Mamun's men proved useless. They cut their way around this plug through the softer limestone to a continuation of the ascending passage. Here the passage is still too low to stand up in and continues on for 129 feet to a level area in the Grand Gallery. Looking straight ahead and level is a route to the Queen's Chamber and above, continuing upward at the same twenty-six-degree angle, is the Grand Gallery that leads to the King's Chamber. It should be noted that these rooms were named—or misnamed—by their Arab discoverers simply because it was their custom to bury their men in a tomb with a flat roof and their women in a tomb with a pitched roof. The names have remained with these rooms to this day. But *The Egyptian Book of the Dead* names them much differently, as we will see later.

The Grand Gallery is nothing short of a masterpiece of planning and engineering. It is 157 feet long and rises to a height of 28 feet over seven courses of masonry. In *Ancient Egyptian Art*, the architects Perret and Chipiez say, "The faces of the blocks of limestone of which the walls are composed have been dressed with such care that it is not surpassed even by the most perfect example of Hellenic architecture on the Acropolis at Athens." Unfortunately, exposure to torches, fumes, and modern air pollution has decayed these vulnerable limestone walls.

At the uppermost end of the Grand Gallery is the Great Step. It rises thirty-five inches to a level platform that begins the entrance to the King's Chamber. Is it mere coincidence that the edge of this great step is exactly in line with the east-west axis at the center of the Great Pyramid itself? Considering the skill of these builders, we should not assume that anything in this structure is coincidental.

Once up the Great Step, one can stand for a short distance, but then must stoop to pass under the first low passage. Next, one encounters an antechamber, but this, too, has a great granite beam one must pass under that comes to within forty-one inches of the floor. At the end of the antechamber one comes to a second low passage, also about forty-one inches from the floor but somewhat longer in length than the first. At last, one enters the King's Chamber, where the air vents and stonework maintain a comfortable sixty-eight degrees year round (that is, before massive tourism raised the temperature).

The King's Chamber is dramatic. Its walls and ceiling are made from a red granite that was mined in the Aswan area some 600 miles upriver from Giza. It is thirty-four feet long, seventeen feet wide, and nineteen feet high. The walls are formed by five courses of stone containing exactly one hundred blocks. The roof is made of nine massive granite beams each twenty-seven feet long and weighing between fifty and seventy tons! As if this isn't amazing enough, five more layers of such beams and intervening spaces lie above the chamber ceiling, finishing in a gabled roof—all of which is presumed to have been designed to protect the King's Chamber from collapse and often referred to as the five "relieving chambers."

Some notes of interest: All nine beams in the King's Chamber have a crack along the southern end, possibly caused by an ancient earthquake. Also, as one author has noted, there are no extra layers of support or roofing above the Queen's Chamber, which, being deeper in the Pyramid, would be subject to greater structural pressures than the King's Chamber. So, why have relieving chambers above the King's Chamber and not above the Queen's? Perhaps the builders were trying to accomplish something other than structural stability when they designed such an elaborate system. Lastly, the sarcophagus is too large to have been placed in the chamber after its completion. This means it was placed there while it was being built, contrary to three thousand years of known Egyptian burial practices. This coffer has also been calculated to have exactly the same interior volume as the Ark of the Covenant. Could it have been used in a manner similar to the Ark; in other words, to contact God?

Much speculation and great effort have been expended in attempting to decipher the mysteries of the Great Pyramid. The majority of those who have studied it closely, however, have concluded that geometry and mathematics are the keys which can unlock its secrets.

The slope of the Great Pyramid differs from all other pyramids in Egypt. This angle—fifty-one degrees, fifty-one minutes—makes the height of the Great Pyramid in proportion to its perimeter at the base exactly the same as the radius of a circle in proportion to its perimeter. This is the well-known value of *pi*, or 3.14. In fact, it has been found that the perimeter of the Great Pyramid is exactly equal to a half minute of latitude at the earth's equator. In addition, it has been shown that the height of the Pyramid corresponds almost exactly to the radius from the center of the earth to the North Pole. The "sacred cubit" seen on the boss in the antechamber to the King's Chamber reflects this measurement and is exactly 1/10,000,000 of this distance! Can this be mere coincidence when we know that the French meter was taken as 1/10,000,000 of the distance of a line drawn from the North Pole to the equator along a meridian that passes through Dunkirk?

The list of mathematical relationships found in the Great Pyramid by its many explorers continues to expand to this day. Some have found evidence for everything from the distance of the earth to the sun, to the mean temperature of the earth itself. What is certain is that a profound intelligence has attempted to preserve and convey knowledge and wisdom to future generations through the construction of this marvelous object. Perhaps nothing is more fascinating to the modern seeker than the possibility that there is something beyond mere data encoded in the Pyramid. Much evidence has been uncovered to suggest that the Great Pyramid also includes a chronology embedded within its very stonework that traces and predicts the course of human activity in the earth. The Edgar Cayce readings agree, stating that the three purposes for the Pyramid are: (1) an initiation for the initiates, (2) a mystical icon throughout the ages, and (3) a chronogram of the transitions that the children of God would go through on their pathway through this dimension. Cayce also says that it is closely connected with a Hall of Records that will be discovered and will reveal the entire story of humanity's experiences.

How can time be recorded in the Great Pyramid? The most important number to come out of the Great Pyramid's geometry is the *pyramid inch;* 365.242 pyramid inches is the geometric circle upon which the design of the Great Pyramid is based. As this number continued to appear in different areas of the structure, it was realized that this was a special measurement. It is the exact number of days in our solar year, and as such it revealed that the Great Pyramid was also a chronogram. One pyramid inch is equal to one year in earth time. With this tool in hand, some researchers have measured the history of humanity, past and future, in the exacting measurements of the Pyramid's floor plan.

Illustration 54 is a diagram by David Davidson which relates earth time to inches within the Great Pyramid.

Explanation of David Davidson's Diagram

The diagram shows how the floor plan is related to historic time. Edgar Cayce reading 5748-6 supports this concept, saying: "In those conditions that are signified in the way through the Pyramid [are the] periods through which the world has passed and is passing, as related to the religious or the spiritual experiences of man . . . " In this same reading, given on July 1, 1932, he said:

> . . . the period of the present is represented by the low passage or depression showing a downward tendency, as indicated by the variations in the character of stone used. This might be termed in the present as the Cruciatarian Age [*cruciat* means "a crusade," and often was used with the words *torturing* or *tormenting,* such as *cruciatory torturing*], or that in which preparations are being made for the beginning of a new sub-race, or a change, which—as indicated from the astronomical or numerical conditions—dates from the latter portion or middle portion of the present fall [1932]. In October there will be a period in which the benevolent influences of Jupiter and Uranus will be stronger, which—from an astrological viewpoint—will bring a greater interest in occult or mystic influences.
>
> At the correct time accurate imaginary lines can be drawn from the opening of the Great Pyramid to the second star in the Great Dipper, called Polaris or the North Star. This indicates it is the system toward which the soul takes its flight after having completed its sojourn through this solar system. In October there will be seen the first variation in the position of the polar star in relation to the lines from the Great Pyramid. The dipper is gradually changing, and when this change becomes noticeable—as might be calculated from the Pyramid—there will be the beginning of the change in the races. There will come a greater influx of souls from the Atlantean, Lemurian, La, Ur or Da civilizations. These conditions are indicated in this turn in the journey through the Pyramid.
>
> How was this begun? Who was given that this should be

a record of man's experiences in this root race? for that is the period covered by the prophecies in the Pyramid. This was given by Ra and Hermes in that period during the reign of Araaraart when there were many who sought to bring to man a better understanding of the close relationship between the Creative Forces and that created, between man and man, and man and his Maker.

Only those who have been called may truly understand. Who then has been called? Whosoever will make himself a channel may be raised to that of a blessing that is all that entity-body is able to comprehend. Who, having his whole measure full, would desire more does so to his own undoing . . .

(Q) What definite details are indicated as to what will happen after we enter the period of the King's Chamber?

(A) When the bridegroom is at hand, all do rejoice. When we enter that understanding of being in the King's presence, with that of the mental seeking, the joy, the buoyancy, the new understanding, the new life, through the period.

(Q) What is the significance of the empty sarcophagus?

(A) That there will be no more death. Don't misunderstand or misinterpret! but the *interpretation* of death will be made plain.

(Q) If the Armageddon is foretold in the Great Pyramid, please give a description of it and the date of its beginning and ending.

(A) Not in what is left there. It will be as a thousand years, with the fighting in the air, and—as has been—between those returning to and those leaving the earth . . .

(Q) What is the date, as recorded by the Pyramid, of entering in the King's Chamber?

(A) '38 to '58. [Notice how Davidson has it as '36 to '53.]

Cayce goes on to say that when we reach the far wall of the King's Chamber, then we are to proceed up the wall, something Davidson never realized. Cayce says in 5748-5 to also notice the variations in stone, color, layers, markings and turns as we make "passage through same . . . from the base to the top—or to the open tomb *and* the top." All of these variations indicate changes in "religious thought in the world."

When Cayce was asked in this reading, "Are the deductions and conclusions arrived at by D. Davidson and H. Aldersmith in their book on the Great Pyramid correct?" he answered, "Many of these that have been taken as deductions are correct. Many are far overdrawn. Only an initiate may understand."

Finally, when asked, "In which pyramid are the records of the Christ?" he answered, "That yet to be uncovered." (5749-2)

9

THE GREAT HALL OF RECORDS

One of the most fascinating and exciting pieces of information to come through Edgar Cayce's visions is the existence of a great Hall of Records, in which are stored the records of our prehistoric descent into matter and the hundreds of thousands of years of activity in the mythological lands of Atlantis, Mu, Lemuria, Og, Oz, Zu, and so on. Actually, Cayce indicates that there are three Halls of Records but that in some magical way they are one.[1] One is in the Yucatan peninsula of Mexico, another in or near Bimini, and the third in Giza, Egypt.

In Yucatan, the record temple is either covered or underground and "overshadowed" by another temple that overhangs it. But Cayce says that it will "rise again." He calls this record temple "the temple by Iltar." According to Cayce, Iltar was a high

---

[1]See Cayce reading 2012-1, paragraphs 29-34 (particularly 31).

priest and leader in Atlantis that led his people on a great migration to the "Aryan or Yucatan land" and there built a temple of records.

In or near Bimini Island in the Bahamas, another record temple is sunken, but Cayce says this temple also "will rise and is rising again." He calls this record temple the temple of "Atlan." As with Iltar, Atlan was a leader who attempted to maintain a temple in Atlantis, but the land changes would not allow it, so his temple sunk with all its records in it for another generation to discover.

The third temple of records is in Giza, Egypt. It is entered by a hall or passageway that begins at or near the Sphinx, according to Cayce. He is inconsistent in his description of it, sometimes referring to it as a "pyramid of records," other times calling it a "temple or hall of records," and on one occasion calling it a "tomb of records." In some discourses Cayce describes its location as being off the right front paw of the Sphinx, in line with the Great Pyramid, which would locate it somewhere east-southeast of the Sphinx. He also references the Temple of Isis, which lies between the Sphinx and the Great Pyramid, as a key to locating the hall or pyramid of records. In another discourse, he clearly states that the record cache is between the Nile and the Sphinx, off its right front paw, in line with the Great Pyramid. On one occasion, he said the shadow of the Sphinx points to the cache. But it seems impossible to cast a shadow across the right front paw when the sun never gets behind the Sphinx's head from the northwest. However, Cayce also said that the poles of the earth were reversed during the ancient times. In which case, the Sphinx would indeed throw a shadow over its own right paw. A mystery yet to be understood.

He also said that the base of the sphinx was "laid out in channels,"[2] and in the left rear corner of the Sphinx, which is facing the Great Pyramid, one can find the wording of how the Sphinx was "founded, giving the history of the first invading ruler [Arart] and the ascension of Araaraart to [Pharaoh]."[3] Accord-

---

[2] 195-14.
[3] *Ibid.*

ing to Cayce, Arart was the first dynasty; Araaraart was the second. They invaded Egypt from Mt. Ararat. It will be an amazing confirmation of Cayce's gift as a seer if these two names are recorded in a corner of the Sphinx.

Cayce clearly says, "as time draws nigh when changes are to come about, there may be the opening of those three places where the records are one, to those that are the initiates in the knowledge of the One God . . . " The time of these changes is not certain, but in his visions Cayce identified the period between 2000 and 2001 as the time of the pole shift, referring to a shifting of the poles of the earth. But there may be several changes over the next many years that could fit his vision. We will see if the pole shift is the one that brings the records to light.

What might be in the Hall of Records? According to Cayce, the Hall of Records contains tablets, linens, gold, and artifacts of import to the cultures that created the record cache. As to the question about what language the records may be in, Cayce did not answer directly. He did say that this was the time when the world spoke one language, a time prior to the Tower of Babel legend in the Bible. Therefore, we could assume that the records in these three locations will be in the same language (although in one reading, Cayce did indicate that the Atlanteans had a slightly different dialect or perhaps pronunciation of the world-wide language than the rest of the world). In one reading, Cayce actually stated that there are exactly "thirty-two of these plates" in the Egyptian Hall of Records that will require interpretation, and this interpretation will take some time. Let's hope it does not take as long as the interpretation of the Dead Sea Scrolls of the Qumran caves.

Cayce says that the records tell the story of the beginnings "when the Spirit took form or began the encasements" in physical bodies in that ancient land of Atlantis.[4] It also includes information about the building of the Great Pyramid.

Yet, when people asked Edgar Cayce if they could be a part of the discovery and interpretation of these records, he would an-

---

[4]378-16.

swer yes, but not necessarily the physical records. As strange as this may seem, according to Cayce, the records are also recorded in consciousness, in the collective mind, and therefore one could open and study the records anytime! Here is an excerpt from one of these strange readings:

> (Q) *How may I now find those records, or should I wait—or must I wait?*
>
> (A) You will find the records by that channel as indicated, as these may be obtained *mentally*. As for the physical records—it will be necessary to wait until the full time has come for the breaking up of much that has been in the nature of selfish motives in the world. For, remember, these records were made from the angle of *world* movements. So must thy activities be in the present of the universal approach, but as applied to the individual.
>
> Keep the faith. Know that the ability lies within self.
>
> 2329-3

From Cayce's perspective, all time is one. There is no space, no time. These are only characteristics of the limited dimension of physical, terrestrial life. Within us is the gateway to oneness, timelessness. The records may be reached by journeying within consciousness, as Cayce did. He never physically went to Egypt, Bimini, or Yucatan. But he so set aside his terrestrial, outer self that he could journey through dimensions of consciousness to the mental Hall of Records. From this perspective, Jesus' statement in John 14:26 that when the Holy Spirit comes, "It will bring all things to your remembrance," takes on a new dimension.

Let's get back to the physical records. If you want to work on seeking the mental records, I've written a different book for that, *Spiritual Breakthrough: Handbook to God-Consciousness.*

Here is one of the most detailed of Cayce's readings on the Atlantis migration to other continents and setting up of temples and record caches. His syntax can be difficult, so take your time, read slowly, deliberately.

Text of Reading 5750-1

[1]Hugh Lynn Cayce: You will give an historical treatise on the origin and development of the Mayan civilization, answering questions.

[2]Edgar Cayce: Yes. In giving a record of the civilization in this particular portion of the world, it should be remembered that more than one has been and will be found as research progresses.

[3]That which we find would be of particular interest would be that which superseded the Aztec civilization, that was so ruthlessly destroyed or interrupted by Cortez.

[4]In that preceding this we had rather a combination of sources, or a high civilization that was influenced by injection of forces from other channels, other sources, as will be seen or may be determined by that which may be given.

[5]From time as counted in the present we would turn back to 10,600 years before the Prince of Peace came into the land of promise, and find a civilization being disturbed by corruption from within to such measures that the elements join in bringing devastation to a stiffnecked and adulterous people.

[6]With the second and third upheavals in Atlantis, there were individuals who left those lands and came to this particular portion then visible.

[7]But, understand, the surface [of Yucatan] was quite different from that which would be viewed in the present. For, rather than being a tropical area it was more of the temperate, and quite varied in the conditions and positions of the face of the areas themselves.

[8]In following such a civilization as a historical presentation, it may be better understood by taking into consideration the activities of an individual or group—or their contribution to such a civilization. This of necessity, then, would not make for a complete historical fact, but rather the activities of an individual and the followers, or those that chose one of their own as leader.

[9]Then, with the leavings of the civilization in Atlantis (in Poseidia, more specific), Iltar—with a group of followers that had been of the household of Atlan, the followers of the worship

of the *One* with some ten individuals—left this land Poseidia, and came westward, entering what would now be a portion of Yucatan. And there began, with the activities of the peoples there, the development into a civilization that rose much in the same matter as that which had been in the Atlantean land. Others had left the land later. Others had left earlier. There had been the upheavals also from the land of Mu, or Lemuria [in the Pacific], and these had their part in the changing, or there was the injection of their tenets in the varied portions of the land—which was much greater in extent until the final upheaval of Atlantis, or the islands that were later upheaved, when much of the contour of the land in Central America and Mexico was changed to that similar in outline to that which may be seen in the present.

[10]The first temples that were erected by Iltar and his followers were destroyed at the period of change physically in the contours of the land. That now being found, and a portion already discovered that has laid in waste for many centuries, was then a combination of those peoples from Mu, Oz and Atlantis.

[11]Hence, these places partook of the earlier portions of that peoples called the Incal; though the Incals were themselves the successors of those of Oz, or Og, in the Peruvian land, and Mu in the southern portions of that now called California and Mexico and southern New Mexico in the United States.

[12]This again found a change when there were the injections from those peoples that came with the division of those peoples in that called the promise land. Hence we may find in these ruins that which partakes of the Egyptian, Lemurian and Oz civilizations, and the later activities partaking even of the Mosaic activities.

[13]Hence each would ask, what specific thing is there that we may designate as being a portion of the varied civilizations that formed the earlier civilization of this particular land?

[14]The stones that are circular, that were of the magnetized influence upon which the Spirit of the One spoke to those peoples as they gathered in their service, are of the earliest Atlantean activities in religious service, we would be called today.

[15]The altars upon which there were the cleansings of the bodies of individuals (not human sacrifice; for this came much later

with the injection of the Mosaic, and those activities of that area), these were later the altars upon which individual activities—that would today be termed hate, malice, selfishness, self-indulgence—were cleansed from the body through the ceremony, through the rise of initiates from the sources of light, that came from the stones upon which the angels of light during the periods gave their expression to the peoples.

[16]The pyramid, the altars before the doors of the varied temple activities, was an injection from the people of Oz and Mu; and will be found to be separate portions, and that referred to in the Scripture as high places of family altars, family gods, that in many portions of the world became again the injection into the activities of groups in various portions, as gradually there were the turnings of the people to the satisfying and gratifying of self's desires, or as the Baal or Baalilal activities again entered the peoples respecting their associations with those truths of light that came from the gods to the peoples, to mankind, in the earth.

[17]With the injection of those of greater power in their activity in the land, during that period as would be called 3,000 years before the Prince of Peace came, those peoples that were of the Lost Tribes, a portion came into the land; infusing their activities upon the peoples from Mu in the southernmost portion of that called America or United States, and then moved on to the activities in Mexico, Yucatan, centralizing that now about the spots where the central of Mexico now stands, or Mexico City. Hence there arose through the age a different civilization, a *mixture* again.

[18]Those in Yucatan, those in the adjoining lands as begun by Iltar, gradually lost in their activities; and came to be that people termed, in other portions of America, the Mound Builders.

[19]Ready for questions.

[20] *(Q) How did the Lost Tribe reach this country?*

(A) In boats.

[21] *(Q) Have the most important temples and pyramids been discovered?*

(A) Those of the first civilization have been discovered, and have not all been opened; but their associations, their connections, are being replaced—or attempting to be rebuilt. Many of the second and third civilization may *never* be discovered, for these would destroy the present civilization in Mexico to uncover same!

[22] *(Q) By what power or powers were these early pyramids and temples constructed?*

(A) By the lifting forces of those gases that are being used gradually in the present civilization, and by the fine work or activities of those versed in that pertaining to the source from which all power comes.

For, as long as there remains those pure in body, in mind, in activity, to the law of the One God, there is the continued resource for meeting the needs, or for commanding the elements and their activities in the supply of that necessary in such relations.

[23] *(Q) In which pyramid or temple are the records mentioned in the readings given through this channel on Atlantis, in April, 1932? [364 series]*

(A) As given, that temple was destroyed at the time there was the last destruction in Atlantis.

Yet, as time draws nigh when changes are to come about, there may be the opening of those three places where the records are one, to those that are the initiates in the knowledge of the One God:

The temple by Iltar will then rise again. Also there will be the opening of the temple or hall of records in Egypt, and those records that were put into the heart of the Atlantean land may also be found there—that have been kept, for those that are of that group.

The *records* are *one.*

[24]We are through for the present.

Let me recap some important parts of the story in this Cayce reading:

Around 10,600 B.C. the great continents of Mu (Lemuria) in the Pacific Ocean and Atlantis in the Atlantic Ocean were in their final stages of destruction; remnant islands were all that was left of their original greatness. Poseidia was the last island of the Atlantean continent. Iltar and Atlan were high priests in the worship of the One God, or Spirit of One. In other readings,

Cayce called these worshipers the "Children of the Law of One." The Yucatan peninsula looked like a good land to migrate to and establish an ongoing community. Iltar and his ten followers did just that. They built altars and temples. On their altars they sacrificed their weaknesses, attempting to make themselves spiritually stronger and purer. They did this by magnetizing large circular stones and then drawing on or evoking the spiritual influences from the One Source.

But there were more earth changes to come, and Iltar's temples and altars were destroyed. In other readings, Cayce recounts that Atlan also lost his temples and altars when Poseidia finally sank.

Yucatan, Central Mexico, Southern California, Arizona, and New Mexico were fast becoming lands of mixed peoples from around the world. The Incas of Peru were also on the move, journeying north to join in the great Mayan development.

The remnant of Iltar's group also journeyed north to become the Mound Builders in the United States.

Over time, the high level of spiritual attunement and worship slipped into self-gratification and glorification, leading to the worship of Baal. Cayce once said that, using the same powers and methods, one could create a god or a Frankenstein; it all depended upon the ideals and purposes motivating the effort.

Around 3000 B.C. remnants of the Lost Tribes of Israel also came to this area of the world. Yucatan, Mexico, the southern U.S., down into western South America were a mix of many influences and ideals, some good and some not so good.

The records of the ancient world and its activities remain in Atlan's cache under the waters off Bimini and in the Yucatan in one of Iltar's covered temples.

An interesting bit of news that adds to this great story comes from a little-known discovery in China in 1900 by a Taoist monk named Wang Tao-Shih. The monk found a hidden ancient library in a series of caves. The texts in this library speak of an ancient time and place in "Motherland Mu." Mu is the original name for the great Pacific Ocean continent of Lemuria, which actually began before Atlantis. Sir Aurel Stein interpreted and reported on these ancient texts in his two titles, *On Ancient Central Asian Tracks* and *Ruins of Desert Cathay*. In 212 B.C., the crazed emperor Chin Shih Huang ordered that all the books and literature relating to ancient China be burned. Whole libraries, including the Grand Royal Library, were destroyed. Chinese literature tells of a semimythical "Five Monarchs" who ruled China during a golden age of wealth and wisdom. This period is considered to have been during the age of the Egyptian Pharaohs, 2852-2206 B.C.

There have been many attempts to discover the Halls of Records in Yucatan, Bimini, and Giza. There have also been discoveries that indicate that the dating of the Great Pyramid and the Sphinx may be too recent and that these monuments may well have been constructed closer to the dates that Cayce gave, 10,500 to 10,450 B.C. Let's begin with the evidence for reconsidering the age of the Giza monuments; then we'll look at some of the discoveries that indicate that there may well be an uncovered Hall of Records.

In 1992, U.S. geologist Robert Schoch, Ph.D., and amateur Egyptologist John Anthony West (author of *Serpent in the Sky*, Harper & Row, 1979) announced to the world press that the age of the Sphinx was much older than originally thought. This revelation sent a shock wave through the international community of professional Egyptologists. In the spring of 1996, in a letter to the Egyptology journal *KMT* (pronounced *k-met*; it is the ancient name for Egypt and means "The Black Land," owing to the rich, black silt left by the Nile after flooding season). In this letter, West outlined his and Dr. Schoch's points:

"1. The Sphinx is not wind-weathered as most Egyptologists think, but water weathered, and by rain;

"2. No rain capable of producing such weathering has fallen since dynastic times;

"3. If it had, other undeniably Old Kingdom tombs on the Giza Plateau cut of the same rock would show similar weathering patterns; they do not;

"Ergo, 4. The Sphinx predates the other Old Kingdom tombs at Giza. Simple as that."

Dr. Schoch estimated the Sphinx to have been constructed from between 5000 to 7000 B.C. "and that the current head of the figure—which everyone agrees is a dynastic head—is almost surely the result of recarving." (*KMT*, Summer 1992, p. 53)

Another date-changing piece of evidence comes from the work of Adrian Gilbert and Robert Bauval, published in their bestselling book, *The Orion Mystery* (Crown, 1994). Actually, the initial ideas about Giza star alignments came from Edgar Cayce, who stated from his trance state in the 1920s that Giza was laid out according to the stars above it. In 1964, Egyptologist Alexander Badawy and astronomer Virginia Trimble published their findings on how the air shafts and passageways in the Great Pyramid aligned with important stars in both the northern and southern heavens. Then, in 1994, Gilbert and Bauval published their findings, identifying many correlations between the stars and structures on the plateau:

1. The three great pyramids of Giza—Menkaure, Khafre, and Khufu—match the stars Mintaka, Al Nilam, and Al Nitak *(delta, epsilon, and zeta Orionis)* located in the belt of Orion. They noted that the third pyramid (Menkaure) is set off from the other two pyramids just as the third star in the belt *(delta Orionis)* is set off from the other two stars.

2. The alignment is most exact in the year 10,500 B.C., the date Edgar Cayce gave for the construction of the Great Pyramid.

3. The star Saiph is over the pyramid of Djedefre, to the north of Abu Ruwash, and the star Bellatrix is over the "Unfinished Pyramid" at Zawyat Al Aryan to the south. When Orion is on the meridian, the star cluster *lambra Orionis,* representing the head of Orion, is over the Dashur pyramids.

4. When Taurus is on the morning horizon, the two pyramids of Dashur, known as the "Red" and the "Bent" pyramids, match the stars Aldebaran and *epsilon Tauri,* the two "eyes" of the bull in the constellation Taurus.

5. The hieroglyphic texts inscribed in the pyramids of Unas (2356-2323 B.C.) and Pepi II (2246-2152 B.C.) refer to the deceased king ascending into the southern skies in the region of the constellation of *Sahu,* which Gilbert and Bauval identify with the constellation Orion. The authors believe that these texts support the idea that there had been some kind of spiritual relationship intended between the Khufu pyramid (the Great Pyramid) and the Orion constellation.

Of all these correlations, the most provocative argument is

the curious and inexplicable "misalignment" of the smaller
Menkaure pyramid with the bigger Khufu and Khafre pyramids,
exactly matching the arrangement of the third star in Orion's
Belt *(delta Orionis)*. If this isn't evidence that the designers, im-
peccable in every other dimension of their work, purposefully
offset the Menkaure because they were laying out the plateau
according to the stars above, then what is the explanation for
offsetting the third pyramid?

A fascinating twist on this alignment discovery is that the
three stars are actually in *reverse* order from the pyramids on
the ground. In other words, the offset pyramid is the southernmost pyramid of the three, while the offset star is the northernmost star of the three. The surprise here is that trance-state
Edgar Cayce identified this, too, saying that the poles were opposite during the building of the Giza plateau! This would mean
that the third pyramid would have been the northernmost pyramid, matching exactly the offset star in Orion's belt! According
to Cayce, the Earth's poles were roughly opposite—north was
south and south was north—during the ancient times. According to him, the planet has and will change its poles. Geologists
have long known about the magnetic shift of Earth's poles, but
Cayce is talking about an axis shift, something geologists do not
agree on. Recently, however, geologists reported that the inner
core of the Earth made a major shift in its axis. Perhaps, as Cayce
predicted, the poles of Earth's crust will also shift again. Cayce
dates this next shift between the year 2000 and 2001!

All of this new star alignment information causes us and the
archaeologists who had their dates so well set to reconsider the
age of the Giza monuments. However, nothing that has been
carbon dated on the Giza plateau gives a dating older than
roughly 3500 B.C., causing one to be careful about jumping on
this 10,500 B.C. bandwagon too soon. The investigation goes on.

Now, let's recount some of the work that has been done in
searching for the record cache, specifically the cache in Egypt.

The director of the Giza plateau has often said that much of
ancient Egypt is still undiscovered. Excavations are turning up
new artifacts all the time. But there is no indication by anything
that has been found that there is a record cache of a civilization
dating back to 10,500 B.C. There is no specific indication that

such exists. Even the texts in the China caves speak only of an ancient motherland, Mu. There are no actual records from Mu in the caves. And, unless we are misinterpreting the hiero- glyphic records that have already been discovered in Egypt, there is no report of an ancient civilization predating the Phara- onic period, of which we have so much evidence. However, the hieroglyphic records do tell that the great Egyptian god Hermes hid his records. This is an important message and has driven many to search for the hidden stash of Hermes. Since he was a god from the original creation time, his records could well tell of pre-Pharaonic ages. His cache may even have artifacts from pre- Pharaonic times. In Edgar Cayce's discourses, Hermes is identi- fied as one of the architects of the Great Pyramid and a key influence in the development of the great Egyptian civilization. Finding his records would certainly be an important step toward finding the Hall of Records. His records may even *be* the actual Hall of Records.

As you may know, Hugh Lynn Cayce, the eldest son of Edgar Cayce, was a major searcher for the Hall of Records. He helped set up the Association for Research and Enlightenment's Egypt Project in the 1970s. At one point, A.R.E. representatives, Egyp- tian authorities, and University of Stanford Research Institute employees were actually drilling into the bedrock of the Sphinx's foundation in search of the Hall of Records. But, as is so often the case, human nature overcame the high purpose of this ef- fort. The owner of the drilling equipment had been told that he would receive his payment in the form of ancient artifacts found in the chamber, probably worth thousands, maybe hundreds of thousands of dollars. But when he was on the site with his equipment, he happened to mention this payment to one of the Egyptian authorities, who informed him that all artifacts belong to the Egyptian people. Upon hearing this, he took his equip- ment and went home. They never drilled any deeper than a few feet. Cayce often said that the records would not be found until the hearts and minds of those seeking were right. In 1970, they were not right.

In 1991, Dr. Schoch and John Anthony West discovered "some indications of cavities and chambers under" the Sphinx. Schoch said that "there's a little cupola on either side; there is definitely what looks on the [refraction] lines like some kind of little chamber or cavities in the vicinities of the cupolas. Definitely, between the paws, you get indications there's some kind of collapsed structure, maybe a collapsed cavity there" (*Venture Inward*, January 1992, p. 17), which were recorded by many microphones set up on the ground around the Sphinx (to pick up the pounding of sledge hammers on steel plates, which generated sound waves). The waves go through the rocks and are picked up by the microphones. Certain forms of refraction of the line of the sound wave indicate open cavities underground rather than solid rock. Professor Schoch wanted more time and money to return to the Sphinx and explore his findings further, but the money never came.

In 1996 and 1997, Dr. Joseph Schor and his colleague, Joseph Jahoda, in coordination with the Schor Foundation and Florida State University, explored the Giza plateau with high-tech ground radar equipment. Dr. Schor reported his initial findings at the annual Egypt conference at A.R.E.'s headquarters in Virginia Beach, Virginia, in 1997. Their ground-penetrating radar indicated that there was a twenty-six-by-forty-foot chamber some thirty feet below the Sphinx. Interestingly, the dream stela in front of the Sphinx shows the Sphinx sitting on top of a chamber. Dr. Schor also reported that there was a passageway running under the Great Pyramid's three Queens' pyramids and then under the Great Pyramid. (*Venture Inward*, September 1997)

As had Dr. Schoch before him, Dr. Schor wanted to recheck and confirm his findings. The following year, he and Joe Jahoda went back to the plateau with more sophisticated ground-penetrating radar and a drilling rig. They drilled a small hole between two of the Queens' pyramids, dropped a camera down the hole, and found what appeared to be a fissure, not a passageway. When they ran the newer radar equipment over this area, it too indicated a fissure, not a passageway. Then, they took the new equipment over to the Sphinx and explored their original findings under the Sphinx. To their surprise, the new radar did not negate the original radar findings, but confirmed them. There is a chamber or series of chambers under the Sphinx. Now, in cooperation with the Egyptian authorities, they are attempting to get permission to once again drill a small hole into the rock under the Sphinx and drop a camera down the hole to see what may be inside the chamber.

Someday, I believe, we will find the Egyptian Hall of Records, and the story these records tell will cause all of us to rethink who we are and what life is really about.